ANATOMY

MADE SIMPLE FOR ARTISTS

JONATHAN FREEMANTLE

Capella

Copyright © Arcturus Publishing Limited
26/27 Bickels Yard, 151-153 Bermondsey Street
London SE1 3HA

This edition printed in 2004 for
Bookmart Limited
Registered Number 2372865
Trading as Bookmart Limited
Blaby Road, Wigston,
Leicester LE18 4SE

ISBN 1-84193-195-0

Printed and bound in China

Contents

Introduction

This book is aimed at anyone who has developed an interest in the use of anatomy for artistic purposes and is looking for a simple, practical introduction into this vast subject. It is important to state that the use of anatomy in drawing, painting or sculpture should be seen strictly as a means to an end.

IT IS A TOOL, ALBEIT A POWERFUL ONE IF CORRECTLY USED, and should not be allowed to obstruct the creative process at all.

The best approach to the study of human anatomy is to use it as a means by which one may understand the movements of the body. The forms created by the movement of the bones, muscles and skin are completely different from when the body is stationary. It is useful to note that at no point in a human life is there no movement in the body; only when the body dies does this movement cease completely.

Because of this it is futile to merely study anatomy by looking at each bone and muscle in a static state; neither is it particularly important for the artist to commit to memory the names of the many muscles and bones in the body.

The artist takes from their enquiry into anatomy only that which serves to strengthen and deepen the power and expression of their art. Any other knowledge is not only superfluous but also potentially destructive.

Another important point to note before embarking on any study of anatomy is that muscles, bones and skin grow and evolve like anything else in life. They are the way they are strictly because of the function they perform. They will also cease to function if they are not used at all. We say: "I'm out of shape" (unfit). We imply that there is a shape that we

could 'be' and due to a lack of exercise (of muscles etc.) have lost that physique. This is a natural process that occurs in every living form. Conversely, if a muscle is over-stimulated through a certain repeated action (exercise) it will react by growing in shape and size.

I have attempted in this book to show that anatomy can be both practical and simple. I have taken life drawings and combined them with anatomical illustrations to shed light on what is going on beneath the surface. The best way to understand anatomy is by creating the need for knowledge. By this I mean that it is much more useful to draw from life, to look at the human body and when a question arises regarding one of the shapes or movements you see in front of you, make a note of it and investigate it anatomically later. This way your study will have purpose and meaning and you are likely to remember what you have learned for next time.

This is where the great difference between possessing information and having knowledge lies. The former is empty and has no focus while the latter comes from direct experience, has life and is personal.

Even the phrase 'to draw' has two very distinct differences in meaning depending on its use. The first use is to describe merely the physical action of drawing (to draw a pencil across a page as an ox draws its plough across the field).

The second use of the phrase is where the real work lies. This use implies drawing from within (to draw water from the well). This is how one should treat all drawing – as a means by which we draw out not only what lies on the surface of our subject, but especially what lies within.

Leonardo da Vinci said:

"A good painter has two chief objects to paint, man and the intentions of his soul; the former is easy, the latter hard, because he has to represent it by the attitudes and movements of the limbs…"

If we are to truly understand anatomy we should also begin to question what it is that makes us move, what does that particular movement that I see before me really mean – beyond the obvious movement by mechanical impulse – and what does it say to me?

For the purposes of this book, it being just an introduction, I have stuck to dealing only with the muscles and bones that have a direct effect upon the surface of the body. For most artists this is all we need.

I would encourage anyone who felt driven to take his or her study further to do so. The journey is as much about understanding the workings of the body as it is about understanding ourselves. Nevertheless, when it comes to the moment of creation, whether it be working from life or imagination, we need to be able to cast off all we have learned, everything we have acquired and meet the task ahead with freshness, vigour and courage to leave behind what is known in favour of the unknown.

A Brief History

Until 1839 and the introduction of the camera, anatomical documentation was 'limited' to the drawings and annotations of artists and men and women of medical science.

THERE HAS ALWAYS BEEN A CLOSE ASSOCIATION BETWEEN ARTISTS and medical science in terms of anatomy. The search for knowledge and understanding of the human body is the same, yet the emphasis is different.

The first accounts of dissections are of those performed by Erasistratus and Aerophilius of the Pholemaic Medical School of Alexandria in 2 BC. After this, evidence is scarce of any further investigation into the workings of the body. This could largely be due to the rise of Christianity and the Christian taboo warning against tampering with the body. During medieval times anyone tampering with the body, or even unduly concerned with the body (which was seen as the rightful property of God only), would end up with eternal hellfire and damnation.

It was only during Italian Renaissance that a marked move away from this attitude took place. In all areas, including as the study of anatomy, the Renaissance produced some startling achievements and advancements. The large shift in thought from the medieval age was in how the human was seen in relation to the divine. This humanist age chose to celebrate beauty of human vessel as a reflection of the perfection of the divine rather than seeing it as an insignificant and impure shell scantily housing the perfect immortal soul.

There are many accounts of Renaissance anatomical research, but none are better than Leonardo da Vinci's (1453–1519) notebooks.

Leonardo da Vinci made extensive studies into the anatomy of the human body and was so ahead of his time that many of his findings are still referred to today as canons of anatomical research.

An equally important aspect of the study of anatomy is proportion. Canons of proportion have formed the framework for artists throughout history - the earliest recorded canons being Egyptian.

The Greeks too had a clearly formulated set of proportions to work by (7.5 heads = body). They believed that man 'being the measure of all things' should be used as a proportional framework for the design of buildings.

Another great artist to investigate the proportions and mechanics of the human form was Albrecht Durer (1471-1528). Working around the same time as Leonardo da Vinci, his two volumes on human proportion go a significant way towards understanding the working of the human form.

The study of anatomy has moved on a great deal since the exciting times of the Renaissance, but the spirit of enquiry has always remained the same. With our now vast knowledge of the human body it would seem a futile study to pick up, yet there is always more to learn and so the ancient study of anatomy carries on.

BASIC ANATOMICAL STRUCTURE

The Skeleton

The skeleton performs three main functions: Support, protection and leverage. Although each person has a different 'build' as determined by the shape and makeup of the skeleton, the basics of function and form are the same within all of us.

There are more than two hundred distinct bones in the adult human body. Each bone is beautifully crafted to perform a specific function and to operate in unison with the bones, muscles and organs that surround it.

The main function of the skeleton is to provide support and protection to the body. Certain bones act as levers for muscles are tailored to hinge so that they can freely move, allowing the muscles to efficiently perform their function. A good example of a bone acting as a lever can be found in the pubic area. Here the Femur meets the pubic bone and hinges at the head of the Femur. The resulting movement (of the leg) is one of the most uniquely human of movements – the ability to stand and walk on two legs.

Other bones are in the place to protect the delicate organs of the body. The skull protects the brain while the ribcage provides protection for the heart, lungs and liver. Some bones have to have a certain amount of flexibility (cartilage) in order for some movement to take place. An obvious example of this would be the ribs, which have to allow for the movement created by the expansion and contraction of the lungs through breathing.

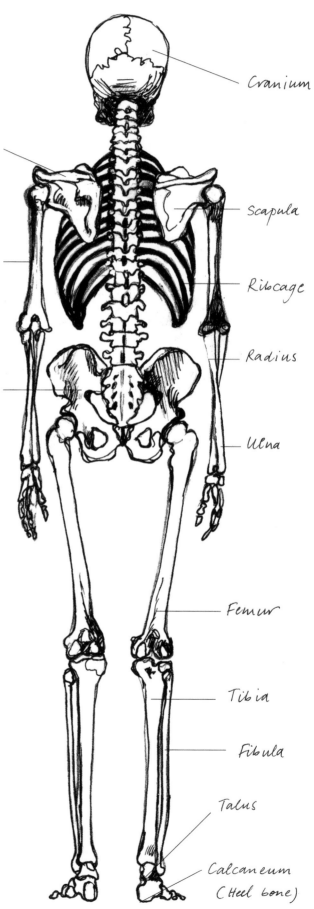

Cranium

Spine of Scapula

Scapula

Humerus

Ribcage

Radius

Pelvic girdle
(Hip Bone)

Ulna

Femur

Tibia

Fibula

Talus

Calcaneum
(Heel bone)

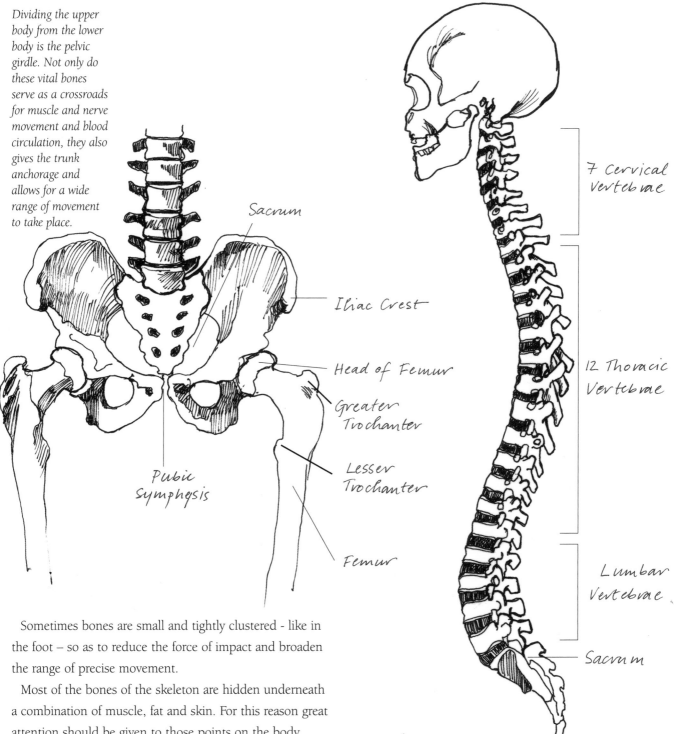

Dividing the upper body from the lower body is the pelvic girdle. Not only do these vital bones serve as a crossroads for muscle and nerve movement and blood circulation, they also gives the trunk anchorage and allows for a wide range of movement to take place.

Sacrum

Iliac Crest

Head of Femur

Greater Trochanter

Lesser Trochanter

Pubic Symphysis

Femur

7 Cervical Vertebrae

12 Thoracic Vertebrae

Lumbar Vertebrae

Sacrum

Coccyx

Sometimes bones are small and tightly clustered - like in the foot – so as to reduce the force of impact and broaden the range of precise movement.

Most of the bones of the skeleton are hidden underneath a combination of muscle, fat and skin. For this reason great attention should be given to those points on the body where bone does obviously show on the surface. These are the key points in any drawing of the figure, the points from which the drawing develops.

It is easy to find these points by using your own body as a guide. By feeling where the bones are on your own body you will gain a more immediate appreciation of the skeletal make-up.

The longest and most intricate range of bones are the bones of the spinal column. The spine is made up of the axis, the atlas, 7 cervical vertebrae, 12 thoracic vertebrae, 5 lumbar vertebrae, the sacrum and the coccyx. The spine and the skull both work together to house the mainframe for the nervous system running throughout the body.

The Muscles

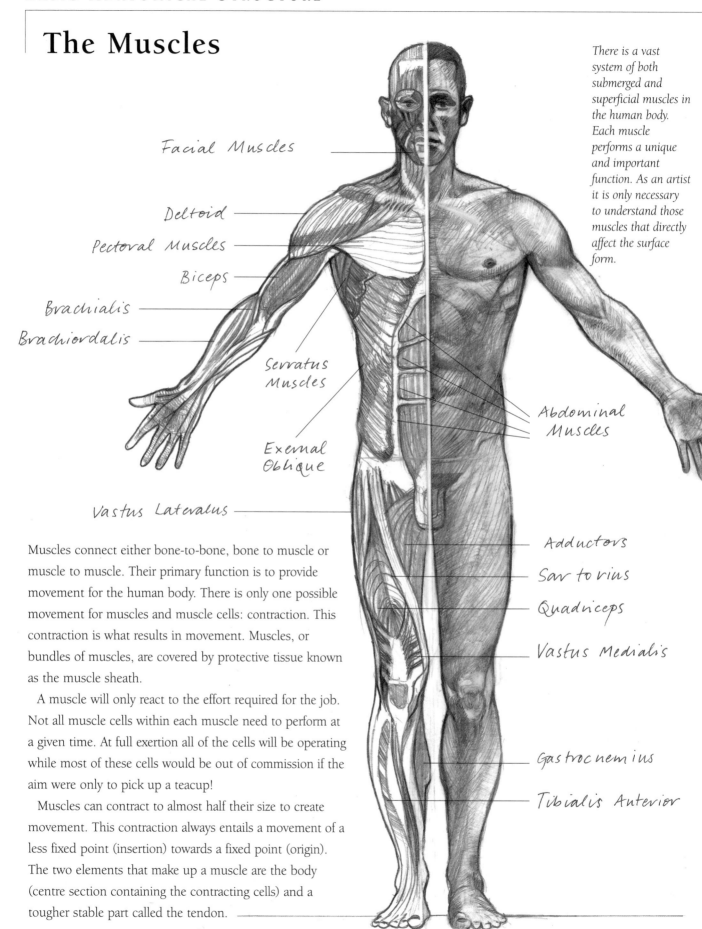

Facial Muscles

Deltoid

Pectoral Muscles

Biceps

Brachialis

Brachiordalis

Serratus Muscles

External Oblique

Vastus Lateralus

Abdominal Muscles

Adductors

Sar to rius

Quadriceps

Vastus Medialis

Gastrocnemius

Tibialis Anterior

There is a vast system of both submerged and superficial muscles in the human body. Each muscle performs a unique and important function. As an artist it is only necessary to understand those muscles that directly affect the surface form.

Muscles connect either bone-to-bone, bone to muscle or muscle to muscle. Their primary function is to provide movement for the human body. There is only one possible movement for muscles and muscle cells: contraction. This contraction is what results in movement. Muscles, or bundles of muscles, are covered by protective tissue known as the muscle sheath.

A muscle will only react to the effort required for the job. Not all muscle cells within each muscle need to perform at a given time. At full exertion all of the cells will be operating while most of these cells would be out of commission if the aim were only to pick up a teacup!

Muscles can contract to almost half their size to create movement. This contraction always entails a movement of a less fixed point (insertion) towards a fixed point (origin). The two elements that make up a muscle are the body (centre section containing the contracting cells) and a tougher stable part called the tendon.

Most muscles connect two bones to each other. This gives leverage and creates the movement of the limbs by a process of expansion and contraction. It is important to understand the function of the muscle and not just its' appearance. This understanding will then communicate through your drawing.

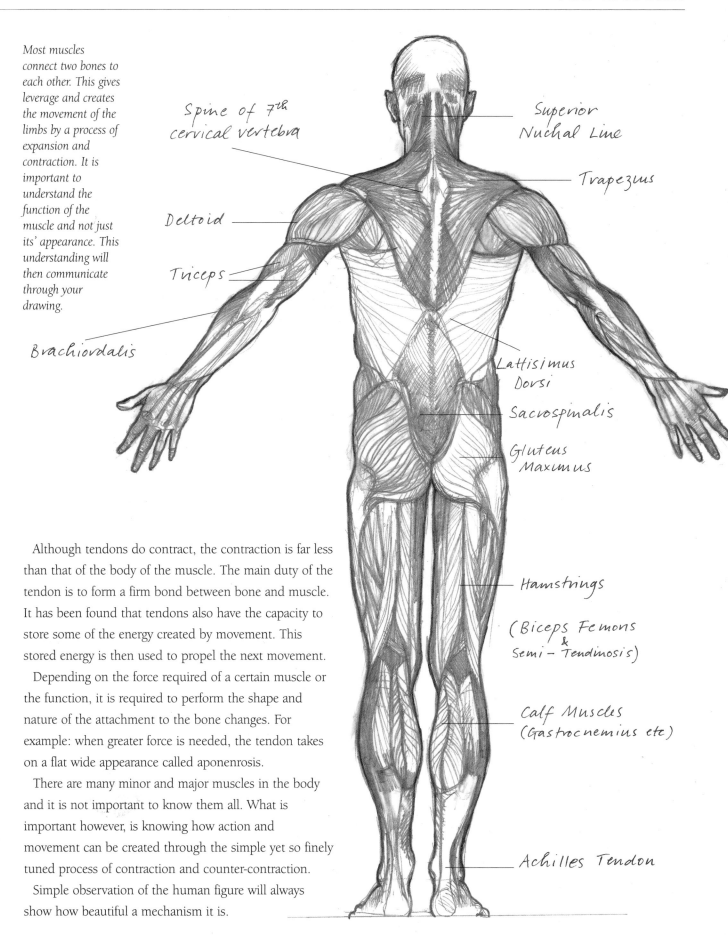

Spine of 7th cervical vertebra

Deltoid

Triceps

Brachiordalis

Superior Nuchal Line

Trapezius

Lattisimus Dorsi

Sacrospinalis

Gluteus Maximus

Hamstrings

(Biceps Femons & Semi - Tendinosis)

Calf Muscles (Gastrocnemius etc)

Achilles Tendon

Although tendons do contract, the contraction is far less than that of the body of the muscle. The main duty of the tendon is to form a firm bond between bone and muscle. It has been found that tendons also have the capacity to store some of the energy created by movement. This stored energy is then used to propel the next movement.

Depending on the force required of a certain muscle or the function, it is required to perform the shape and nature of the attachment to the bone changes. For example: when greater force is needed, the tendon takes on a flat wide appearance called aponenrosis.

There are many minor and major muscles in the body and it is not important to know them all. What is important however, is knowing how action and movement can be created through the simple yet so finely tuned process of contraction and counter-contraction.

Simple observation of the human figure will always show how beautiful a mechanism it is.

ANATOMY
IN PRACTICE

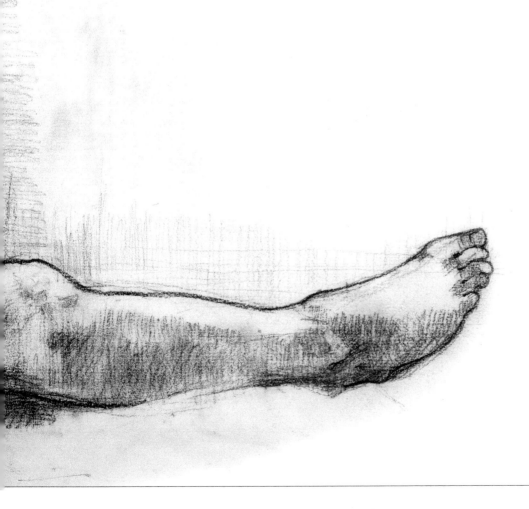

The Head

NOWHERE MORE THAN WITH THE HEAD DO THE BONES SO obviously shape the surface form. There is also nowhere else in the body that has such a high concentration of muscle action. Each facial expression requires a combination of many minor and major facial muscles.

There is only one movable joint in the head however, the jaw. The jaw is completely separate from the skull and joins at the mastoid process.

The movement of the jaw is controlled largely by a muscle called the masseter. This powerful muscle not only holds the lower jaw, but is also used for chewing. We can often feel the masseter tire or stiffen when we have been chewing excessively on something.

Two other vital muscles are those that control the opening and closing of the eyes and mouth. These muscles form a complete circle and can therefore contract considerably. This contraction is important since muscles control the opening of two vulnerable points where the inner body is exposed to the surface. These muscles are known as Oibicularis Oculi (eye) and Orbicularis Oris (mouth) and are termed sphincters due to the function they perform.

The contraction of the frontalis muscle that covers the frontal bone results in the raising of the eyebrows and the folding of the skin on the forehead. When we are surprised or shocked, the expression we assume will often involve these muscles, hence we say, 'to raise an eyebrow.'

Certain other facial muscles are known for the main expression for which they are responsible. The grinning muscle or risorius pulls the orbicularis oris (mouth) muscle towards the ear and hence causes what we know as a grin.

The smiling muscles or zygomaticus, major and minor, pull the corner of the mouth diagonally upwards towards the top of the ear. These muscles work with the risorius to create a smile.

When the muscles controlling the movement of the lower lip during contraction are combined with the flanking movement in the depressor labii, a frown is created. The movement of lips and mouth also has the fundamental function of articulating sound and speech. All of the previously mentioned muscles are used for this as are the levator muscles (levator labii, levator angulious and levator labii alaeque nasi), which pull upwards on the top lip.

When drawing the eyes it is very important to remember that they are essentially balls in a socket (a mistake often made when drawing eyes is the tendency to make them look flat).

This socket is the orbital cavity. The ball of the eye rests in this socket and is protected by it. The eye is then covered by the obicularis oculi muscle, which controls the opening and closing of the lid over the eye.

The ridge that runs just below the eyes, popularly called the cheekbones (zygomatic arch) is another subterranean landmark worth nothing when drawing the face. On certain people it is more pronounced or angular whilst on others it is less so, although it remains a distinctive feature on each individual nevertheless.

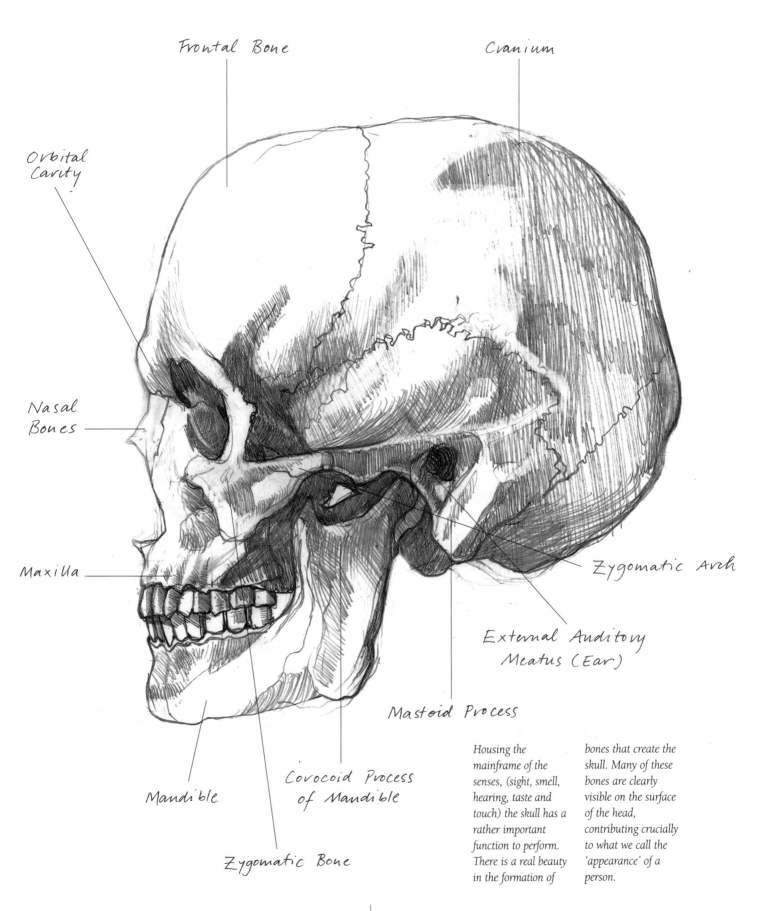

Frontal Bone

Cranium

Orbital Cavity

Nasal Bones

Maxilla

Mandible

Zygomatic Bone

Corocoid Process of Mandible

Mastoid Process

External Auditory Meatus (Ear)

Zygomatic Arch

Housing the mainframe of the senses, (sight, smell, hearing, taste and touch) the skull has a rather important function to perform. There is a real beauty in the formation of bones that create the skull. Many of these bones are clearly visible on the surface of the head, contributing crucially to what we call the 'appearance' of a person.

The Head

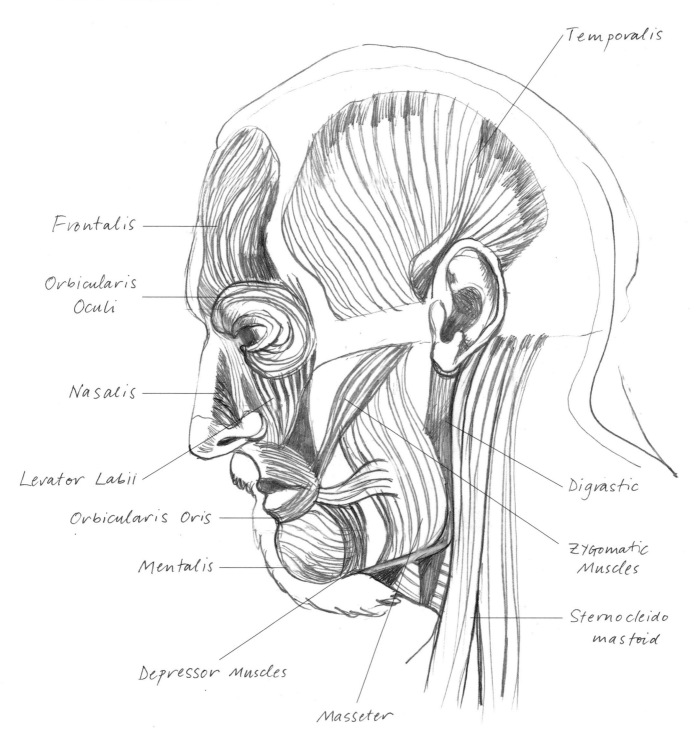

Temporalis

Frontalis

Orbicularis
Oculi

Nasalis

Levator Labii

Orbicularis Oris

Mentalis

Digrastic

Zygomatic
Muscles

Sternocleido
mastoid

Depressor Muscles

Masseter

The substructure of the face is made up of a wide range of major and minor, deep and surface muscles, all of which contribute to the remarkable range of expression possible with the human face. Although every face is different the muscles underneath the skin are all of the same make up. In different people different muscles will be more or less developed. Muscles have 'memory' so if a certain movement is repeated often enough the muscle will remain fixed in that position. Hence we have 'happy' looking people and 'moody' people for example.

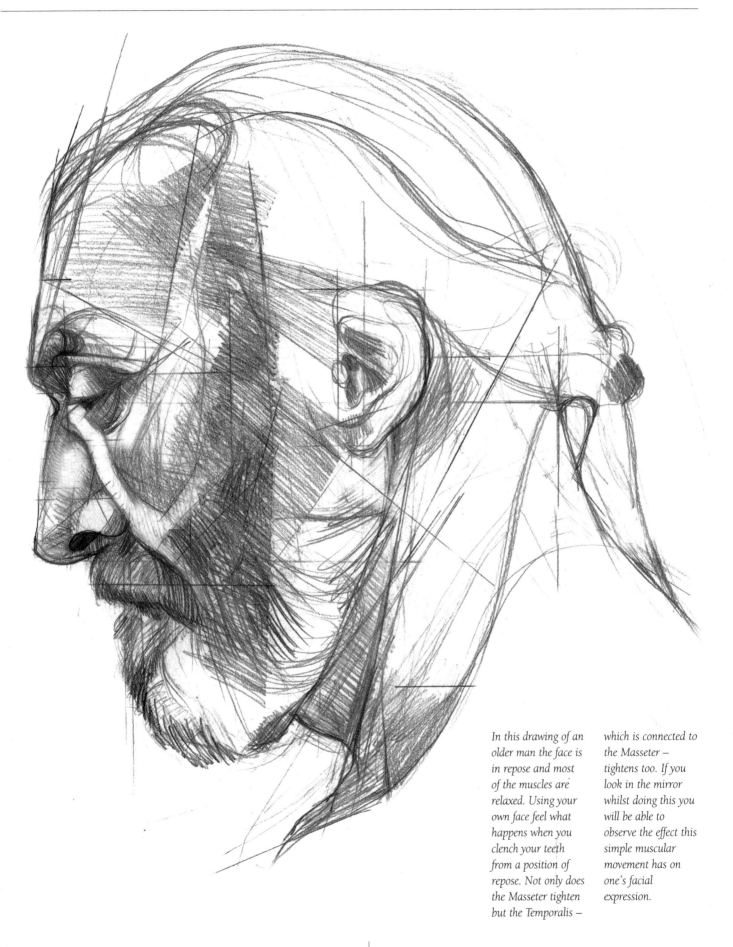

In this drawing of an older man the face is in repose and most of the muscles are relaxed. Using your own face feel what happens when you clench your teeth from a position of repose. Not only does the Masseter tighten but the Temporalis – which is connected to the Masseter – tightens too. If you look in the mirror whilst doing this you will be able to observe the effect this simple muscular movement has on one's facial expression.

The Neck

Within the neck are the vocal cords. The tone or pitch of the voice changes according to the length of these cords. These cords resonate in the wind passage (with its origin in the lungs) to create sound. This sound is then regulated and given articulation by the movement of the tongue, mouth and lips. This is the miracle process that allows us to speak, sing, laugh and scream.

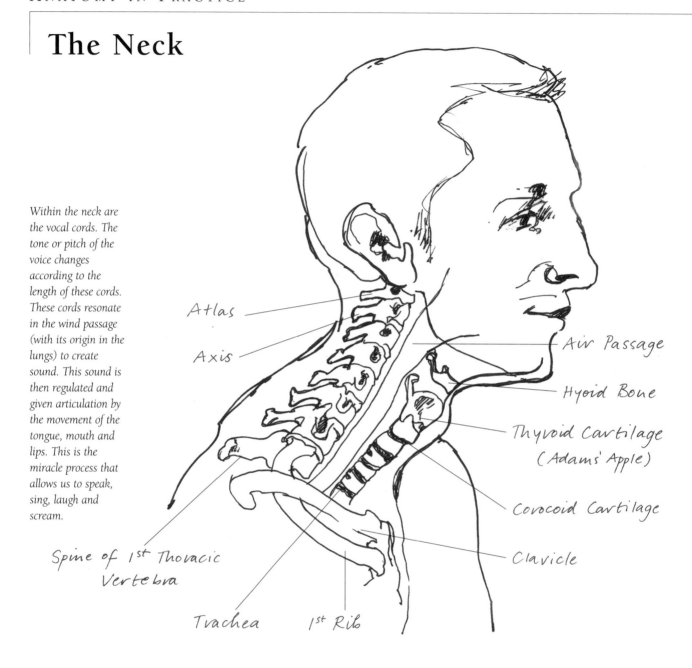

Atlas

Axis

Air Passage

Hyoid Bone

Thyroid Cartilage (Adams' Apple)

Coricoid Cartilage

Clavicle

Spine of 1st Thoracic Vertebra

Trachea   1st Rib

THE MOST PRONOUNCED MUSCLE VISIBLE ON THE SURFACE OF THE neck is also the most powerful of the neck muscles, the sternomastoid. Running along the front of the neck is a column containing the air passage. Within this column are the thyroid bone, the thyroid cartilage, the coricoid cartilage and the trachea. The thyroid cartilage and the muscles around it contain the vocal cords. This also forms what we know as the Adam's apple, which is more pronounced in the male.

The name originates from the story of Adam and Eve where Adam eats the apple given to him by Eve from the forbidden tree of the knowledge of good and evil. Some of this apple became lodged in Adam's throat, creating a lump.

The spinal vertebrae in the neck are smaller than in the rest of the spine to allow for more versatility of movement. They curve to create the forward thrust of the head. This curve is called the cervical curve.

The vertebrae are held firmly together by strong ligaments, which in the neck are called ligamentum nuchae. These ligaments are also attached to the rear base of the skull and form the tough fibrous sheet at the back of the neck casing the muscle of this area – postvenor triangle.

Although there is great strength in the neck, it is also an area of considerable vulnerability.

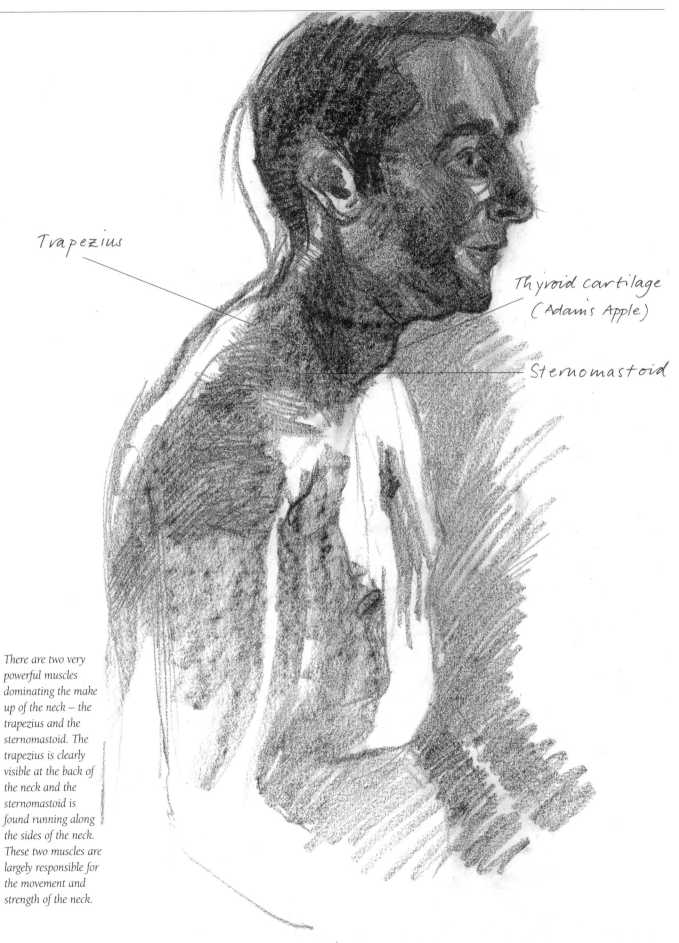

Trapezius

Thyroid cartilage
(Adam's Apple)

Sternomastoid

There are two very
powerful muscles
dominating the make
up of the neck – the
trapezius and the
sternomastoid. The
trapezius is clearly
visible at the back of
the neck and the
sternomastoid is
found running along
the sides of the neck.
These two muscles are
largely responsible for
the movement and
strength of the neck.

The Spinal Column and Rib Cage

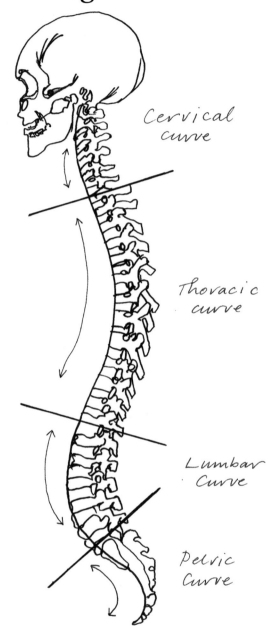

Cervical curve

Thoracic curve

Lumbar Curve

Pelvic Curve

THE SPINE IS MADE UP OF FIVE SECTIONS OF VERTEBRAE. IN TOTAL the spine consists of twenty-four vertebrae which are divided thus: the coccyx and the sacrum (pelvic curve), the five lumbar vertebrae (lumbar curve), the twelve thoracic vertebrae (thoracic curve) and seven cervical vertebrae (cervical curve).

Although each vertebra differs in size and appearance, they all share the same basic design. They are all designed to perform in unison in creating the framework of the body. In between each vertebrae (excluding the first two cervical vertebrae) is an articular disc. This disc acts as a shock absorber and keeps the vertebrae from grinding into each other. One of the most common forms of back pain occurs when one of these discs is worn down or slips out of place (slipped disc) exposing the spine to extra pressure.

Connected to the vertebrae at the articular facet are the ribs. Ribs come in pairs that join at the sternum and the spine to form a ring. Together the ribs form a cage-like shape to protect the lung, heart and liver. The rib cage is the largest structure of the human body. There are usually twelve pairs of ribs in the adult body, however a thirteenth single rib, or pair, is not uncommon. The first ten pairs of ribs are joined in the front of the body to the breast bone (sternum) by a moveable but strong substance called cartilage. This cartilage allows for the expansion and contraction of the chest during breathing.

The breast bone (breast plate) has three sections. This division into three again allows for expansion during breathing. Each of the ribs are linked by the internal and external intercostal muscles. These muscles seal the spaces between the ribs and are responsible for respiration (breathing).

Perhaps two of the most prominent bones visible on the surface of the body are the collar bones (clavicle). They link the upper breast-plate (scapula) at the acromio-clavicular joint. Because no muscle obscures the collarbones they are easy to see and it is simple to chart their movement as the shoulder and arm moves.

Most of the muscles of the neck, chest and arm are in some way connected to the clavicle. The clavicle also works in close union with the scapula and together they are some of the body's most mobile muscles.

There are four curves to the spine. These curves are more or less exaggerated from person to person and give the general drama and rhythm of the body. The cervical curve gives the thrust of the neck and head. The thoracic curve is the longest and often the least dramatic. The lumbar curve gives the arch of the lower back and the pelvic curve counter-balances the lumbar curve moving in the opposite direction into the pelvis.

The Back

THE BACK IS MADE UP OF A MYRIAD OF MUSCLES, MOSTLY attached to the spine, many of which are hidden underneath the surface muscles. Not only do these muscles allow for actions such as lifting and the twisting of the torso, they are also responsible for the vital function of keeping the upper body upright. Often, through either laziness or habit, we adopt a poor posture – and expect the muscles of the back to perform unnatural actions. This can lead to severe back pain. Another major cause of bad posture and back pain is when the muscles of the stomach are weak through lack of use. This weakness transfers the weight of the upper body onto the muscles of the back, effectively leading to an overload. Apart from the subter-ranean muscles, there are three very distinctive surface muscles which are immediately visible when we look at the back. These are the Trapezius, the Latissimus Dorsi and the Sacrospinalis.

The Sacrospinalis run along the full length of the spine and can be seen on the surface as two ridges on either side of the spine. The Sacrospinalis begins at the sacrum and the Iliac Crest. This attachment creates an indentation at the base of the spine and the resulting dimples are one of the most characteristic features visible on the lower back. The Sacrospinalis is divided into three component muscles; the shortest and closest to the spine is the spinalis muscle and links the upper Lumbar and lower cervical spines.

The next muscle, the Longissimus, links the skull, the vertebrae, ribs, sacrum and pelvis. The Ilio-Costo-Cervicals link the pelvis and sacrum with the neck and is attached to the vertebrae and ribs.

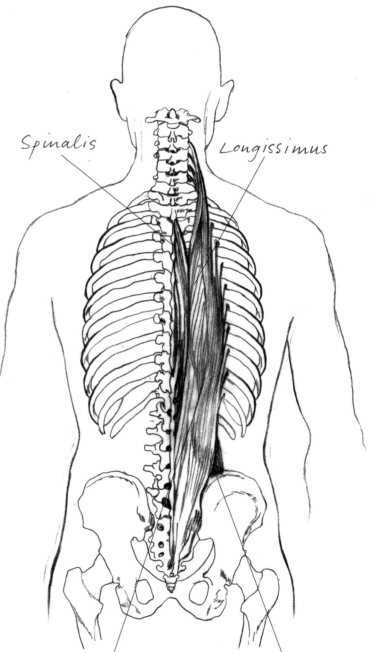

Spinalis

Longissimus

Ilio-costo-Cervicals   Quadratus
Lumborum

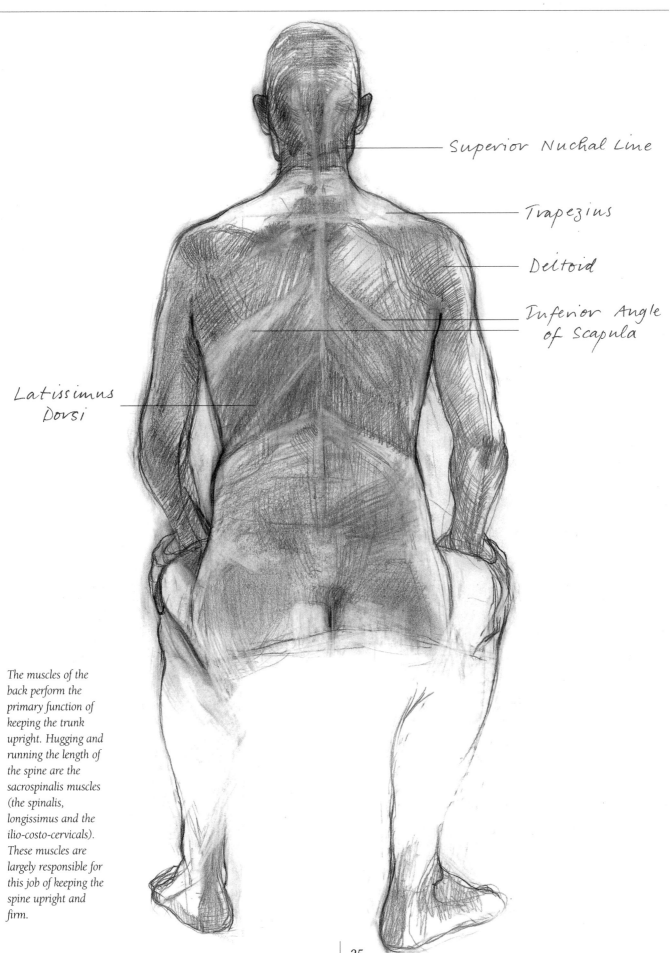

Superior Nuchal Line

Trapezius

Deltoid

Inferior Angle
of Scapula

Latissimus
Dorsi

The muscles of the back perform the primary function of keeping the trunk upright. Hugging and running the length of the spine are the sacrospinalis muscles (the spinalis, longissimus and the ilio-costo-cervicals). These muscles are largely responsible for this job of keeping the spine upright and firm.

25

The Back

BEFORE DESCRIBING THE FUNCTION OF THE TRAPEZIUS, it is important to address the function of one of the most important surface bones, the Scapula. The triangle shaped Scapula (shoulder blade) is one of the most mobile of bones and is capable of moving up and down the spine, to the left and the right as well as rotating. As the Scapulae move over around the upper region of the back the changes in shape and appearance are marked. The spine of the Scapula is a pronounced ridge running along the top of the range of back muscles (the Trapezius being the largest of these muscles). This spine is always visible since it is so pronounced and the forms an excellent anchor to any drawing of the back.

The Trapezius is a muscle spanning the shoulders and the back of the neck ending at a point half way down the back at the twelfth Thoracic Vertebrae.

Because the Trapezius moves in three directions, this muscle has a great deal of mobility. The Trapezius muscle controls most of the forward thrust and backward pull of the shoulders and provides support to the Pectoral girdle when a heavier-than-normal weight is being carried. The clavicle (collar bone) forms the skeletal connection between the Scapula (shoulder blade) and the Pectoral girdle.

The third major back muscle which is important when you wish to understand the 'look' of the back is the Latissimus Dorsi. This powerful muscle connects to the back from the seventh Thoracic vertebrae, down the vertabrae of the spine and includes the Lumbar and Sacral vertebrae. The Latissimus Dorsi also attaches to the lateral edge of the Iliac Crest with its upper insertion of the Latissimus Dorsi formed at the Humerus. It controls all of the backward movements of the arm, as well as rotating the Humerus forward in its socket and brings the arm towards the body.

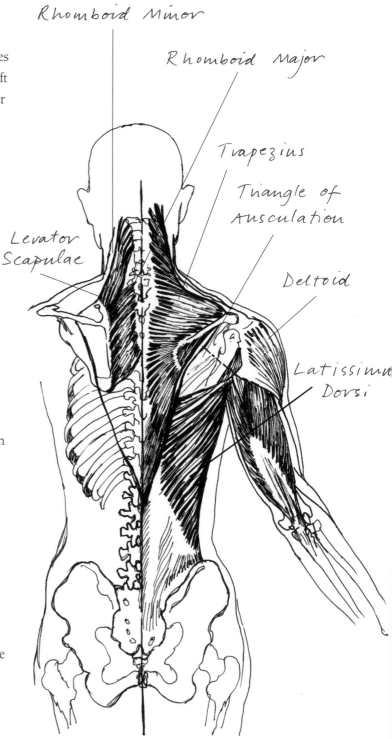

Rhomboid Minor

Rhomboid Major

Trapezius

Triangle of Ausculation

Levator Scapulae

Deltoid

Latissimu Dorsi

When we look at the
female back we are
usually more aware of
the skeletal
'landmarks' on the
surface. Of particular
interest to the artist
are those points - such
as the two dimples
created by tendon
hugging the spines of
the iliac crest – that
give the back its
'character'. It is vital
also when drawing the
back that close
attention is given to
observing the curve or
twist of the spine.

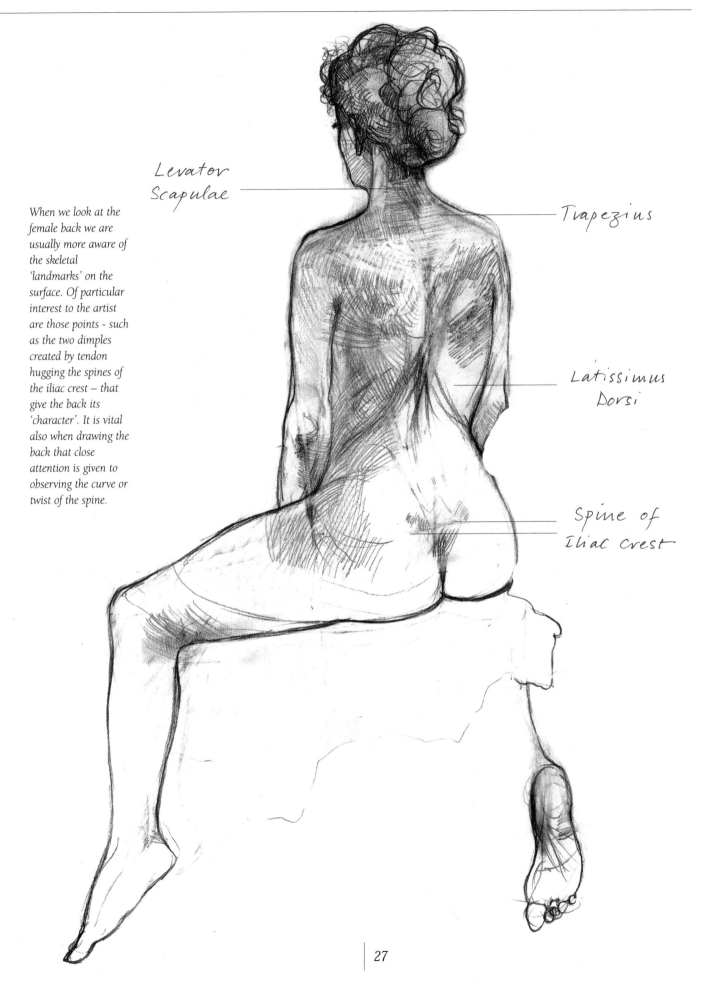

Levator
Scapulae

Trapezius

Latissimus
Dorsi

Spine of
Iliac Crest

The Chest

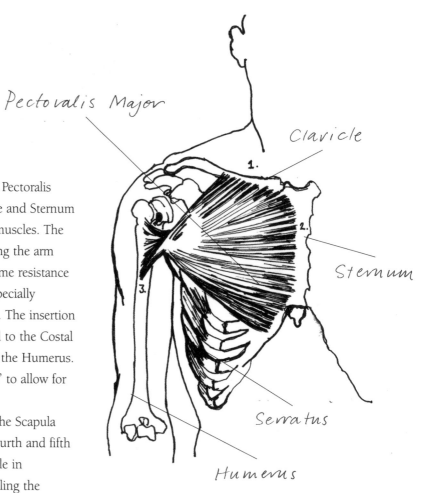

THE TWO MAJOR MUSCLES OF THE CHEST ARE THE
Pectoralis Major and the Pectoralis Minor. The Pectoralis
Major connects the Humerus with the Clavicle and Sternum
as well as the fifth and sixth Costal Cartilage muscles. The
main function of the Pectoralis Major is to bring the arm
towards the body and allow it to flex when some resistance
is applied. Its insertion into the Humerus is specially
tailored to allow greater movement of the arm. The insertion
is twisted so that the muscle bundles attached to the Costal
Cartilages are at the highest point possible on the Humerus.
When the arm is lifted up, this twist 'unravels' to allow for
greater extension.

The Pectoralis Minor attaches to a ridge on the Scapula
called the Corocoi Process and to the third, fourth and fifth
ribs. The Pectoralis Minor has an important role in
increasing the extension of the arm and in pulling the
shoulder forward. In the sport of cricket the fast bowler
relies heavily on this muscle to give pace to his delivery.

Running along the side of the upper trunk (following the
ribs) are the Serratus Anterior muscles. These muscles have
their fixed attachment (origin) on the upper nine ribs and
insertion on the inner side of the Scapula. Because they run
along the ribs they are often mistaken in drawings for ribs,
but on closer observation it can be seen that they run at
slightly different angles. These short intense muscles
perform actions such as pushing and punching and along
with the Pectoralis muscles are more developed on the male
than on the female.

Lying on top of the Pectoralis muscles on both males and
females are breasts or Mammary Glands which on the male
are small and functionless. The breasts attach to the body
by ligaments held inside the skin of the chest and perform
no muscular function. Female breasts begin to develop at

The pectoralis major muscle has three points of attachment to the skeleton. 1. The clavicle. 2. The sternum. 3. The humerus. This powerful muscle (along with the deltoid, biceps and trapezius) gives strength and control to the movements of the arm.

puberty and lower and flatten at the top. The Mammary
Glands enlarge when a woman is pregnant and for a time
after birth when they produce milk. The fat surrounding the
Mammary Glands is what gives the breasts their shape and
is also what accounts for the variation in size of female
breasts.

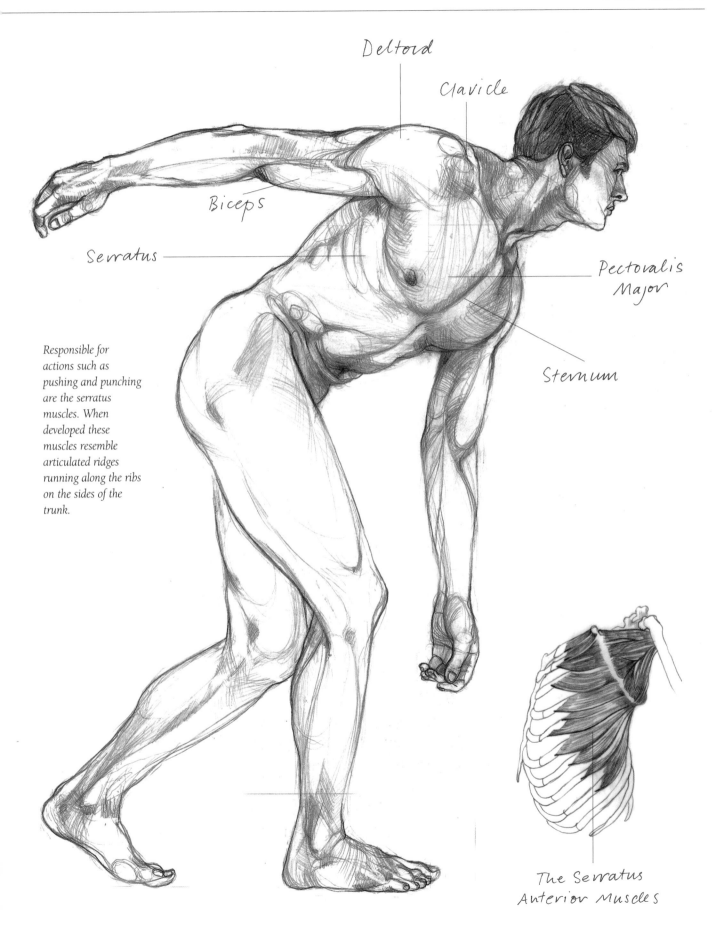

Deltoid

Clavicle

Biceps

Serratus

Pectoralis Major

Sternum

Responsible for actions such as pushing and punching are the serratus muscles. When developed these muscles resemble articulated ridges running along the ribs on the sides of the trunk.

The Serratus Anterior Muscles

The Upper Arm

THERE IS ONLY ONE BONE IN THE UPPER ARM, THE Humerus. This powerful, long bone has two articulated ends with its upper end forming a joint with the Scapula. This joint is important in that it is the origin of all movement in the arm and has thus been tailored in such a way as to allow maximum movement. Movement is made possible by the shallow socket of the Scapula, and the head of the Humerus, which is approximately one third of a sphere, being connected.

The lower end of the Humerus has two articulated areas. The first fits into a socket on the Radius (one of the two bones of the lower arm), the other forms a joint with the second bone of the lower arm, the Ulna. These two articulations of the lower Humerus can be easily seen and felt as they are usually very pronounced.

The three main muscles of the upper arm are the Deltoid, the Biceps and the Triceps. Other muscles include the Brachialis and the Corobrachialis. The Deltoid is attached to the Clavicle, the Scapula and Acromion, connecting it to the body. It inserts into the Humerus of the Deltoid tuberosity (see page 26) and is divided into three parts which all perform distinct functions. The first controls the flexion of the arm, the second the extension and the third the raising of the arm.

The three major muscles of the upper arm are the deltoid, the biceps and the triceps. These three muscles are largely responsible for vital actions such as lifting and pulling.

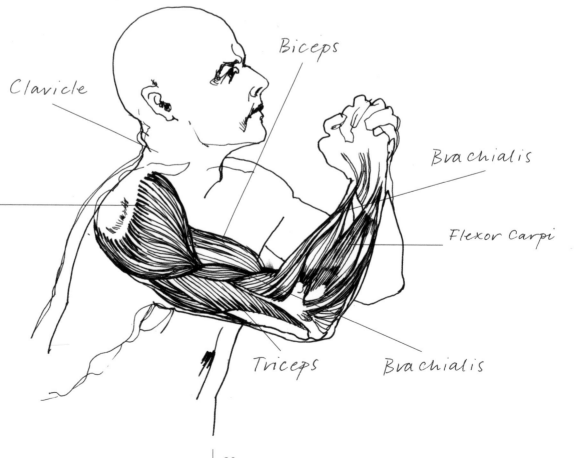

Clavicle

Biceps

Brachialis

Deltoid

Flexor Carpi

Triceps

Brachialis

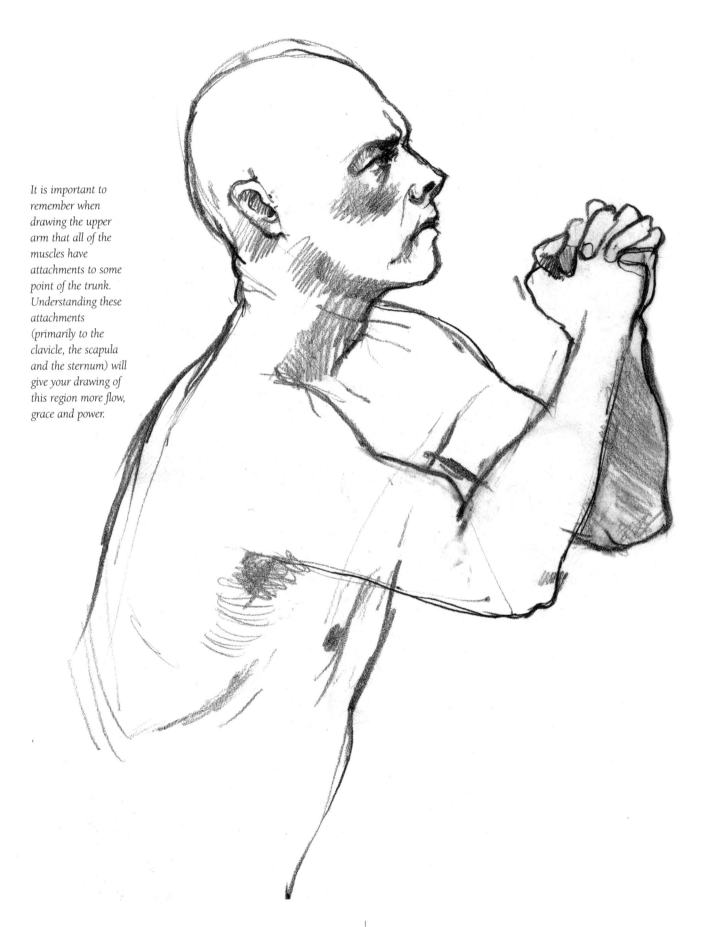

It is important to remember when drawing the upper arm that all of the muscles have attachments to some point of the trunk. Understanding these attachments (primarily to the clavicle, the scapula and the sternum) will give your drawing of this region more flow, grace and power.

The Upper Arm

THE BICEPS PULLS THE FOREARM TOWARDS THE SHOULDER DURING contraction and has tremendous potential for a relatively small muscle when strengthened. At its origin the Biceps muscle is split into two heads of strong tendon. One of these tendinous heads is attached to the Scapula, the other (the shorter of the two) is attached to the Corocoid Process. The insertion of the Biceps is at the Radius of the lower arm. This insertion is what allows the lever action of the arm as the Biceps pulls the forearm towards the shoulder during contraction.

The Triceps muscle runs along the underside of the upper arm. The Triceps has three tendinous heads at its origin (long, medial and lateral). The long head attaches to the lower section of the Scapula. The medial and lateral heads both attach to the underside surface of the Humerus. The insertion of the Triceps muscle spans from around the middle of the Humerus right up to the upper region of the olecranon at the elbow.

Lying underneath the Biceps muscle and adding its bulge in both flexion and contraction is the Brachialis. With its origin along the shaft of the Humerus and its insertion into the Ulna, the Brachialis performs a similar function to the Biceps and works in unison with it.

There are four smaller muscles with their origin along the Scapula and connecting to the upper part of the Humerus: the Supraspinatus, the Infraspinatus, the Teres Major and the Terse Minor. Running underneath the Deltoid, the lower Trapezius and the upper Latissimus Dorsi, these muscles help operate the rotation and backward and forward movement of the shoulder and upper arm. These muscles can affect the surface as well by causing an extra bulge in the Deltoid and Latissimus Dorsi depending on the movement and pressure placed on the arm and shoulder.

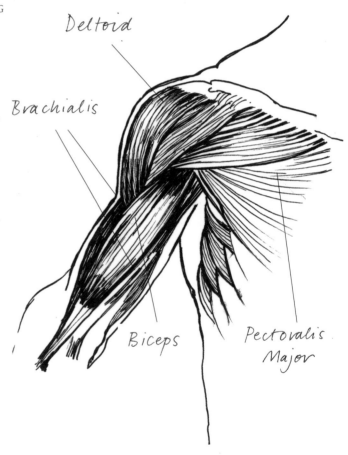

Deltoid

Brachialis

Biceps

Pectoralis Major

It is important to remember when drawing the upper arm that all of the muscles have attachments to some point of the trunk. Understanding these attachments (primarily to the clavicle, the scapula and the sternum) will give your drawing of this region more flow, grace and power.

The Lower Arm

THE MUSCLES OF THE LOWER ARM ARE MANY AND COMPLEX. Their main function is to perform varied and completely essential movements of the hand. Most of the muscles of the forearm have their body in the upper regions and are connected to the hand with long cable-like tendons, of which there are over twenty passing through the wrists. This powerhouse cluster of over thirty muscles, including the Flexor Digitorum Profundus, the Brachiordalis, the Flexor Carpi Radialis, the Flexor Pollicis Longus, the Flexor Digitorum Sublimis, the Palmaris Longus, the Extensor Digitorum, the Extensor Carpi Radialis Brevis, the Extemsor Carpi Ulnaris and the Abductor Pollicis Longus, all work together to give power to the movement and grip of the hand. So many unique muscles are necessary in this area simply because the fingers (and thumbs) need independent, as well as group, functionality.

The three groups of muscles (with joined tendons) are as follows: the first is the long extensor muscles that run along the front of the arm supinating the palm and extending the wrist, fingers and thumb (i.e. they pull the hand open). The second is the Flexor muscles that run along the underside of the arm and end up in the palm - these muscles control the flexion (grip) of the wrist, fingers and thumb. The third group of muscles are those found in the palm and are technically muscles of the hand. These muscles are what gives mass to the hand and flex, extend, adduct and abduct the fingers and thumb.

The Supinator, the Pronator Teres and the Pronator Quadratus all allow the palm of the hand to rotate backwards and forwards. The Flexor Pollicis Longus controls the flexion of the thumb, while the Flexor Digitorum Profundus inserts into the four fingers with long tendons (all with their origin in the same muscle) and controls the flexion of the tips of the fingers.

Responsible for changing and lifting and easily visible in the upper region of the forearm (particularly during contraction) is the Brachiordalis. Connecting the Humerus and the Radius, it adds great strength to the elbow joint and lever mechanism of the arm.

Without the thumb, the hand would almost be unable to clasp and grip, two of its primary functions. For this reason the muscles in the lower arm that operate the thumb are of real importance; rotating the thumb outwards is the Abductor Pollicis Longis, extending the thumb backwards is the Extensor Pollicis Brevis whilst pulling the thumb inwards - and the strongest of the three muscles - is the Extensor Pollicis Longus. These three muscles work together in giving the thumb the strength to perform its vital duty for the human body.

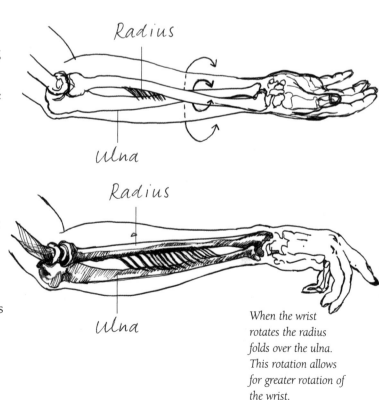

When the wrist rotates the radius folds over the ulna. This rotation allows for greater rotation of the wrist.

Controlling the grip of the hand (creating the clenched fists in this drawing) are the flexor muscles. These muscles have long tendons that run into the hand while the meat of the muscle is collected around the upper region of the lower arm. They are very easy to locate if you feel the change in size and tension of this region with one hand while clenching your fist with the other.

Muscles of the Stomach (Abdomen)

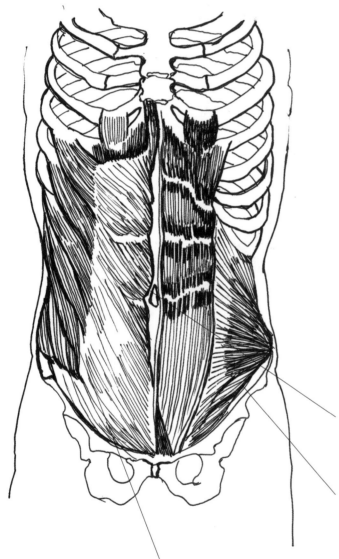

The Rectus Abdominus

Transversus

Exernal Oblique Muscles

THE STOMACH IS (PARTICULARLY WITH THE FEMALE BODY) SUCH A major area for fleshy build up that its muscles are often hidden well below layers of fatty tissue. In fitter men we often say we can see his 'six-pack,' referring to the stomach muscles. The six-pack is, in fact, an eight-pack since there are four intersections of muscle on each of the two straps of the Rectus Abdominis muscle. The two straps are attached into the Cartilages of the fifth, sixth and seventh ribs and span all the way to the Pubis on the front underside of the Pelvic Girdle; the aponeurosis tendon that runs vertically between the two straps of the Rectus Adominis is called the Linea Alba.

This line runs down the centre of the lower chest and stomach and is key when drawing the human figure as it gives an anchor to the eye as well as providing the artist with a useful 'third profile'. The belly button lies along this line and also gives the artist an excellent landmark from which to work.

The rectus abdominus muscles are used to pull the torso towards the legs (pulling the body up from lying down to sitting upright).

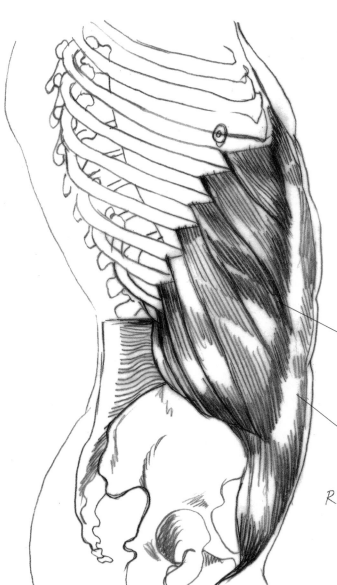

Flanking the Rectus Abdominis on either side are the External Oblique, the Maternal Oblique and the Transversus muscles. These muscles perform the function of rotating and bending the trunk forward. The tendons of these muscles, due to the flattened nature of their attachment to the ribcage create a sheet of flat blended diagonal muscle on either side of the stomach. These muscles connect the rib cage and the upper ridge (Costal Margin) of the Pelvis. The External Oblique forms the external layer with the Internal Oblique running underneath; the male Scrotum is formed out of the Aponeurosis of these three muscles. This culmination in the Pubis creates the triangular appearance of the abdomen so characteristic to the look of the human build.

Controlling the twist of the torso and assisting the action of the rectus abdominus muscles are the external oblique, internal oblique and the transversus muscles. It is the external oblique muscles that we see most clearly however since they are the largest of the three and are closest to the surface.

The External oblique Muscles

Rectus Abdominus

Muscles of the Stomach (Abdomen)

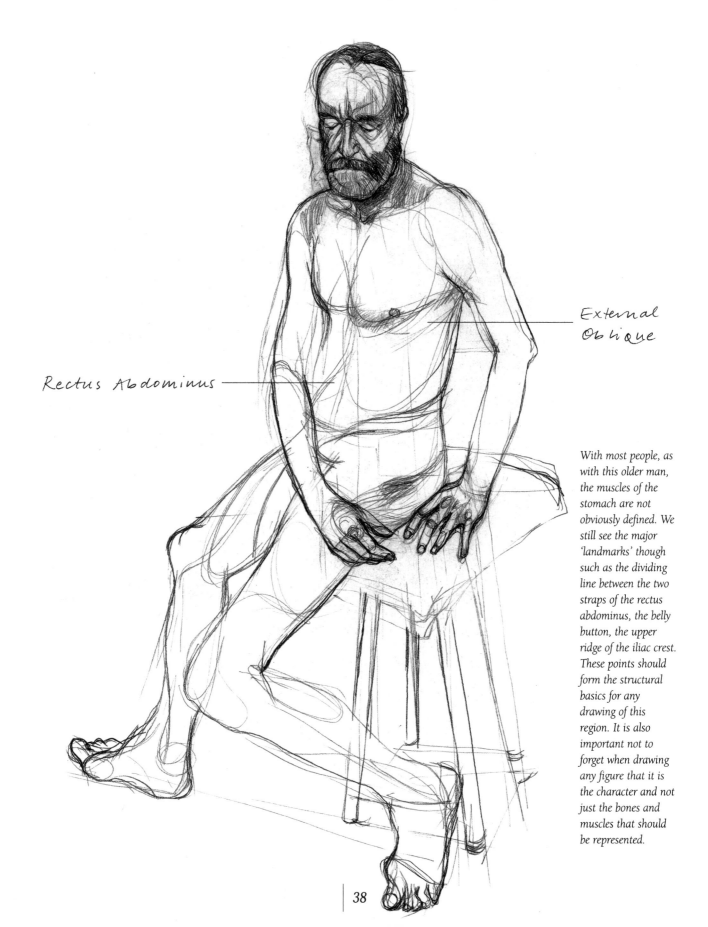

External Oblique

Rectus Abdominus

With most people, as with this older man, the muscles of the stomach are not obviously defined. We still see the major 'landmarks' though such as the dividing line between the two straps of the rectus abdominus, the belly button, the upper ridge of the iliac crest. These points should form the structural basics for any drawing of this region. It is also important not to forget when drawing any figure that it is the character and not just the bones and muscles that should be represented.

38

Look for the energy and flow in the figure you are drawing. In these drawings I have taken just the basic flow and energy of the figure and have chosen not to represent the details of anatomical structure.

The Pelvis

THE PELVIC AREA IS LARGELY GIVEN ITS APPEARANCE BY THE highly characteristic Pelvic Girdle with its two wing-like hipbones. The Pelvic Girdle is a powerful anchor linking the upper and lower sections of the body. Because of this there are few local minor muscles but only muscles arriving and departing, its graceful shape dictated by the needs of these journeying muscles.

The male and female Pelvic Girdles differ greatly. Due to the needs of childbirth, the female Pelvic Girdle is wider than the male; during the process of giving birth the female Pelvis widens even further at the Symphesis Pubis. The female Pelvis is also tilted more further forwards than the male. This tilt has the effect of making the female rear more pronounced and arching the lower back slightly more than the male. Another effect of this extra tilt is to expose the Sacrum and Coccyx thus accentuating the movement of the hips in the female.

The three main differences between the male and female pelvis are as follows: 1. The hips are wider in the female 2. The female pelvis is tilted forward while the male pelvis is tilted backwards 3. The male pelvic girdle is more triangular in shape when seen from the posterior and anterior aspect (front and back)

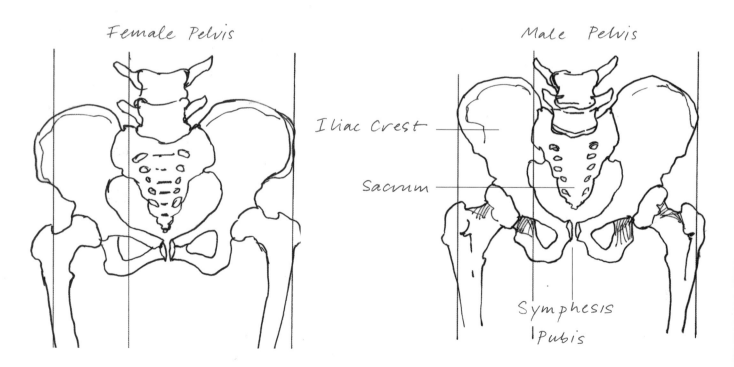

Female Pelvis

Male Pelvis

Iliac Crest

Sacrum

Symphesis Pubis

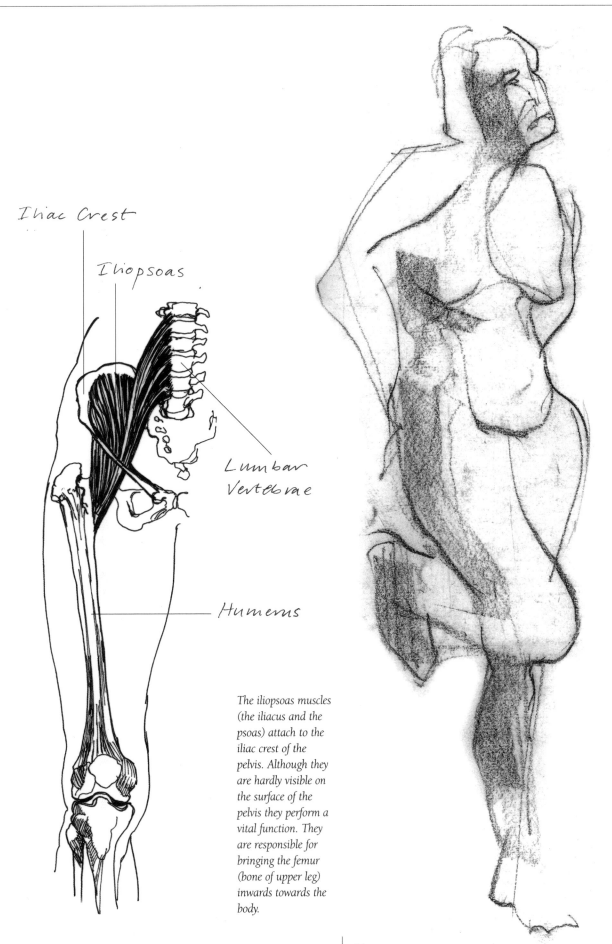

Iliac Crest

Iliopsoas

Lumbar
Vertebrae

Humerus

The iliopsoas muscles
(the iliacus and the
psoas) attach to the
iliac crest of the
pelvis. Although they
are hardly visible on
the surface of the
pelvis they perform a
vital function. They
are responsible for
bringing the femur
(bone of upper leg)
inwards towards the
body.

41

The Pelvis

In this drawing the focus is on the flow of the form with the emphasis being placed on the pelvic region. Particular attention is given to the 'triangle' formed when connecting the dimples created by surfacing of the iliac crest and vertebrae of the lumbar region of the spine.

The Gluteus Muscles and the Muscles of the Thigh

THE LARGEST OF THE GLUTEUS MUSCLES AND ONE OF THE MOST powerful of all of the muscles of the body is the Gluteus Maximus. This large rhomboidal muscle has a wide origin on the Iliac Crest, the Sacrum and the Coccyx and runs all the way down to the Femur. We can clearly see the shape of this muscle since it is so large and is always in use. This muscle is most intensely used for actions such as climbing stairs, walking, running etc.

The smaller of the Gluteus muscles, the Gluteus Medius and the Gluteus Minimus, also have their origin on the Iliac bone. Their insertion is higher on the leg though, in the Great Trochanter. These muscles are responsible for lifting the leg sideways and rotating the leg forward, when kicking for example.

The main muscles linking the Pelvic Girdle with the Femur are the Iliopsoas Pectineus, the Adductor Longus, the Rectus Femorus and the Sartorius. Most of these muscles will be discussed as part of the function of the upper leg, but it is worth noting here the function of the Iliopsoas muscle. Composed of two muscles, the Iliacus and the Psoas, this muscle pulls the leg (Femur) towards the body. The Iliopsoas also connects both the lower spine and the Pubic Girdle to the Femur. Although it is largely a subterranean muscle, its influence is significant on the shape of this region.

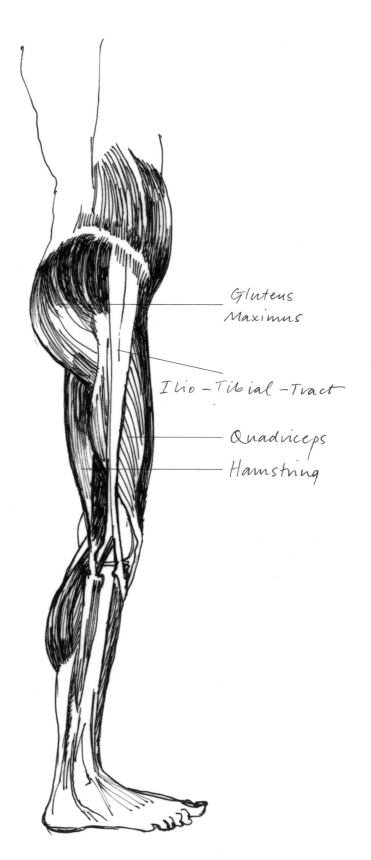

The powerful gluteus muscle connects the pelvic girdle and the femur. This muscle is used in fundamental actions such as climbing and running.

Gluteus Maximus

Ilio-Tibial-Tract

Quadriceps

Hamstring

It is interesting to observe how function can change form. Because birds travel by air and the flapping their wings it is natural that the strongest or most developed muscle in their anatomy is the Pectoral (breast) muscle. Humans, as we know, propel themselves by walking or running, so naturally the Glutens and other related muscles are bigger and more developed.

It may seem obvious to mention this here but it is well worth remembering what is mentioned earlier in the book: that every bone and muscle is how it is because of what it does. The more we look at the function of the components of the body, the more we realise how perfect and in order everything is.

In this loose drawing we see the gluteus muscle in flexion (a relaxed state). Because the weight is almost entirely placed on the right leg the muscles on this region are forced upwards and the hip is thrust side wards. This emphasis forms the major movement in the classical renaissance ideal human stance known as 'contraposto'.

Contraposto or 'counter balance' is created by the thrust of the hips being balanced out by an opposite angle and thrust of the shoulders. We can see evidence of this even in this drawing by observing that the right shoulder is lower and closer to the hips then the left, thus balancing the thrust of the hips.

The Upper Leg

THE MAIN FUNCTION OF THE LEGS IS TO CREATE THE FORWARD propulsion of the body (walking, running, jumping etc). The muscles and bones of the leg therefore are designed to perform this function with endless possibilities. The two powerhouse muscles of the upper leg are the Quadriceps and the Hamstrings. The Quadriceps (or Quadriceps Femoris) muscles run along the front of the leg and is composed of four muscles all of which work together to lift and rotate the leg.

These four muscles are the Rectus Femoris, the Vastus Laturalus, the Medalus and the Intermedius. The Rectus Femoris helps the Iliopsoas in the flexion of the hip as well as connecting to and pulling on the Patella (kneecap). The Vastus Laturalus, the Medalus and the Intermedius work all with the Rectus Femorin the extension of the knee (walking etc) as well as serving to stabilize the knee during all movement.

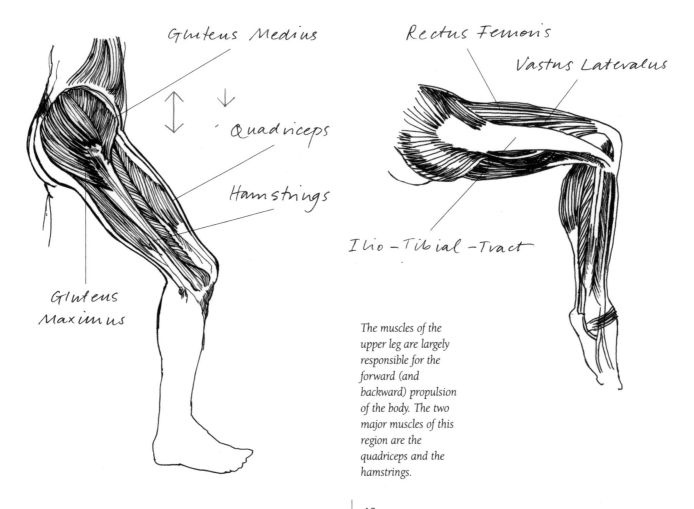

The muscles of the upper leg are largely responsible for the forward (and backward) propulsion of the body. The two major muscles of this region are the quadriceps and the hamstrings.

The Upper Leg

THE HAMSTRING MUSCLE HAS THREE COMPONENT PARTS. THESE muscles connect at their origin to the Ischial Tuberosity of the Pelvis and to the shaft of the Femur. They are called the Biceps Femoris, the Semimembransus and the Semitendinosus. Together the Hamstring muscles pull the lower leg back towards the body. Together with the Glutens muscles the Hamstrings work to allow for climbing and running. They are seen on the surface of the leg as strong cables linking the hips with the rear of the knee. Tendinous outcrops are formed where muscles join the Tibia and Fibula and are the tendons that, when severed, prevent any movement of the legs ('Hamstrung').

The third major muscle of the leg is also the longest muscle in the body. The Sartorius is a narrow seatbelt-like strap that moves diagonally across the front of the leg linking the Arterior Superior spine and the upper shaft of the Tibia. During contraction the Sartoris adducts and rotates the thighs and bends the knee.

Another similar long, thin muscle, the Gracilis, adducts the thigh, rotates the leg medially and flexes the knee. The

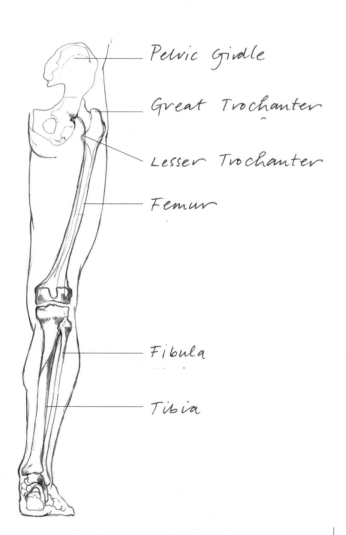

Pelvic Girdle

Great Trochanter

Lesser Trochanter

Femur

Fibula

Tibia

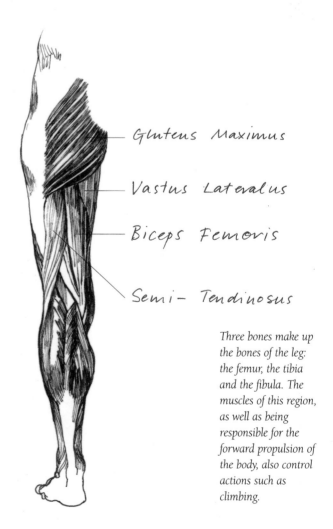

Glutens Maximus

Vastus Lateralus

Biceps Femoris

Semi- Tendinosus

Three bones make up the bones of the leg: the femur, the tibia and the fibula. The muscles of this region, as well as being responsible for the forward propulsion of the body, also control actions such as climbing.

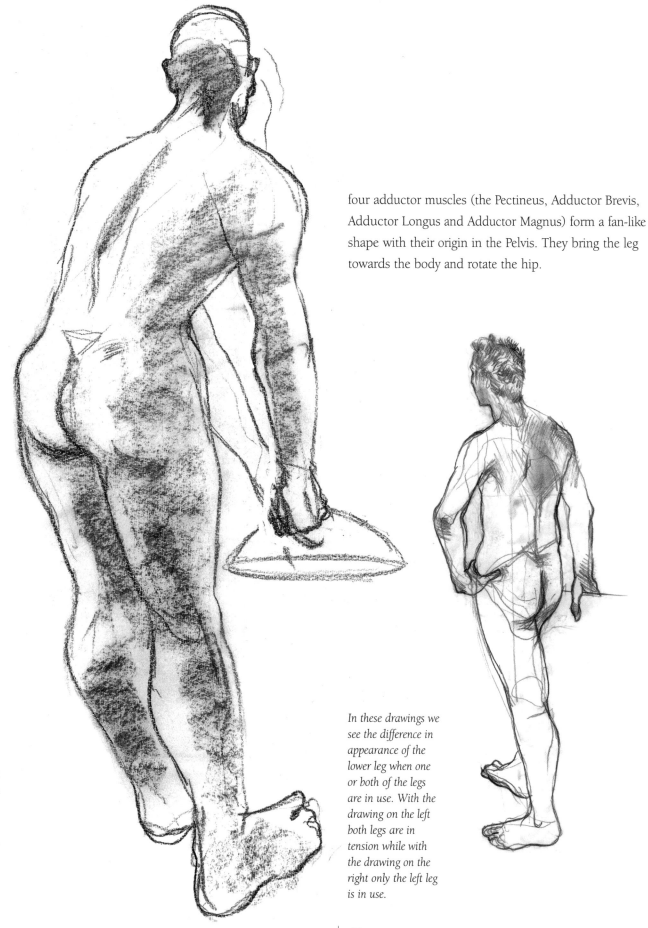

four adductor muscles (the Pectineus, Adductor Brevis, Adductor Longus and Adductor Magnus) form a fan-like shape with their origin in the Pelvis. They bring the leg towards the body and rotate the hip.

In these drawings we see the difference in appearance of the lower leg when one or both of the legs are in use. With the drawing on the left both legs are in tension while with the drawing on the right only the left leg is in use.

49

The Knees

THE KNEE IS THE POINT AT WHICH THE HUMERUS JOINS THE large Tibia of the lower leg. On the front of this joint is the kneecap (Patella), an independent bone whose function is to help the easy passage of the Quadricep tendons over the knee. The joint of the knee is formed by the 'balls' or Medial and Lateral Condyles of the Femur slotting into the Medial and Lateral Condyles of the Tibia (which are recessive and concave).

It is well worth paying particular attention to the knee joint as its function is so vital to movement of the leg. Also, since it is such a large joint and has very little muscle and fat surrounding it, we can have a very clear idea of the subterranean structure of the knee just by looking at the surface. The knee is also the most vulnerable joint of the body and is usually the most susceptible to injury.

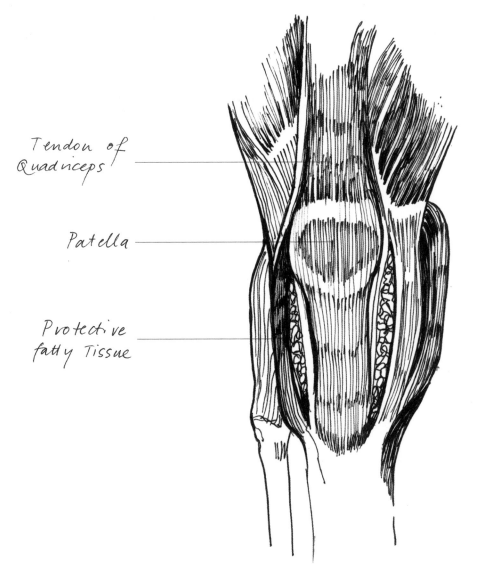

Tendon of
Quadriceps

Patella

Protective
fatty Tissue

We can see clearly in this illustration how the powerful tendon of the quadriceps stretches tightly over the patella and connect to the head of the fibula. The patella (kneecap) is in primarily in place to perform the function of assisting the stretch of this tendon over the knee region.

The Lower Leg

Lateral Condyle of Femur

Head of Fibula

Head of Tibia

Tibia

Fibula

Lateral Malleolis

Tarsals

Phlanges

Calcaneus

Meta tarsals

OF THE TWO BONES IN THE LOWER LEG (THE TIBIA AND THE Fibula) the Tibia is far stronger and bigger. The smaller Fibula hinges in the underside of the Tibial tuberosity and flanks the outer side of the Tibia running to just below the Malleolis of the Tibia. This lower connection is what creates the outside ankle (Lateral Maleolis). The head of the Fibola can also usually be seen as a bump on the lower exterior of the knee.

The lower leg is made up of a great number and variety of long, thin muscles which lead into the foot as powerful cable-like tendons. The muscles of the lower leg can be divided into two categories: the first running down the front of the leg along the skin, and the other running behind thus forming the calf muscle and its tendinous tributaries. These muscles work to keep balance and propel the body forward by giving power and poise to the movement of the foot.

The main muscle responsible for creating the flexion of the foot (lifting the foot) is the Tibialis Arterior, with its origin at the Lateral Condyle and the upper Lateral shaft of the Tibia. This muscle narrows as it passes down the leg into a long tendon; this tendon passes under the instep of the foot with the insertion under the foot also allowing for an inward turn of the foot.

The major bone of the lower leg is the tibia with the lesser fibula flanking it on the outer side if the leg. These bones angle inwards from the knee. This bow of the bones is from time to time exaggerated in people. This extra 'bow' of the legs is knows as being 'bow-legged.'

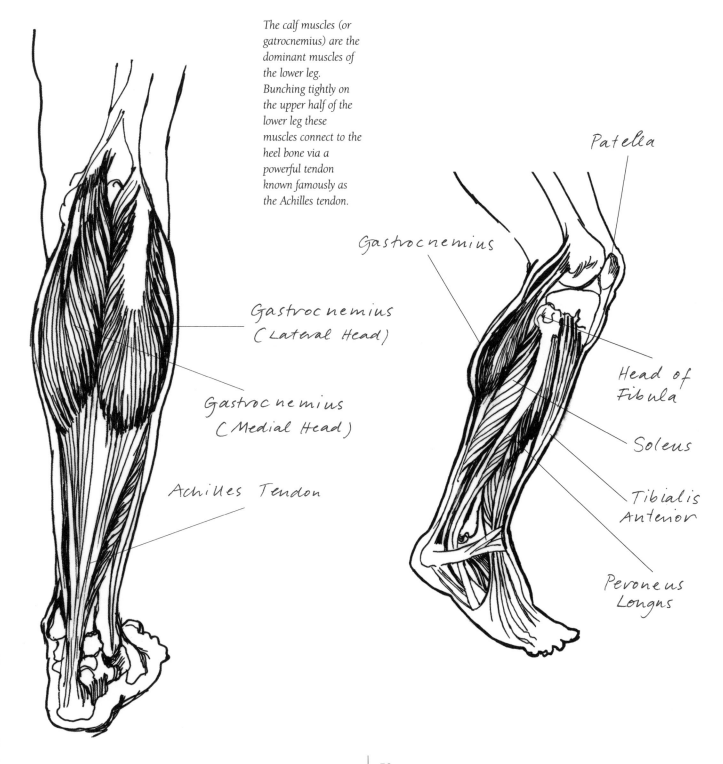

The calf muscles (or gatrocnemius) are the dominant muscles of the lower leg. Bunching tightly on the upper half of the lower leg these muscles connect to the heel bone via a powerful tendon known famously as the Achilles tendon.

Patella

Gastrocnemius

Gastrocnemius (Lateral Head)

Gastrocnemius (Medial Head)

Head of Fibula

Soleus

Tibialis Anterior

Achilles Tendon

Peroneus Longus

The Lower Leg

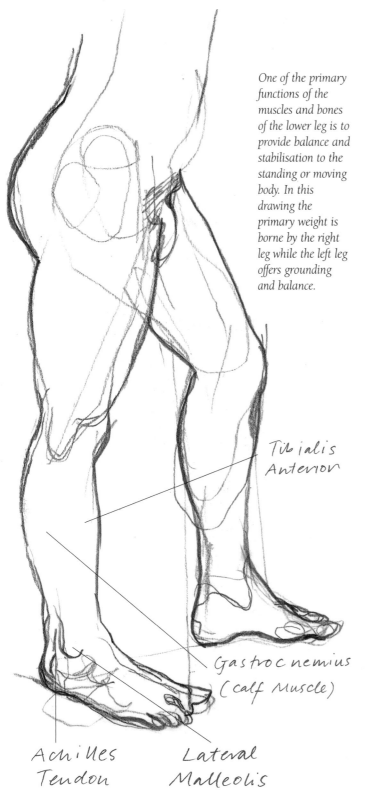

Tibialis Anterior

Gastrocnemius (calf Muscle)

Achilles Tendon

Lateral Malleolis

One of the primary functions of the muscles and bones of the lower leg is to provide balance and stabilisation to the standing or moving body. In this drawing the primary weight is borne by the right leg while the left leg offers grounding and balance.

Another powerful muscle running down the front of the lower leg is the Extensor Digitorum Longus. This muscle arises from the Lateral Condyle of the Tibia. As it passes down the leg it divides into four parts thus connecting the lateral four toes and pulling them back against the foot. These tendons are clearly visible on the roof of the foot when this contraction occurs.

Other muscles of the anterior (front) aspect of the lower leg include the Peroneus Longus and Peroneus Tertius, the Extensor Itallicus Brevis, the Extensor Digitorum Brevis and the Extensor Hallicus Longus.

The function of the Extensor Hallicus Longus with its origin beneath the Tibialis is to extend the big toe. When the big toe is lifted we can clearly see this tendon protruding. You can get an idea of the strength and power of this muscle and tendon if you feel it in tension. It is also of vital importance as it is the big toe that works most heavily in order to stabilize the standing body.

The largest superficial muscle running down the back of the lower leg is the Gastrocnemius or calf muscle. The flesh of the muscle is bundled at the upper part of the leg and as the muscle moves downwards it soon becomes tendon. This tendon bends with the tendon of another muscle, the Soleus, and becomes the Achilles tendon.

Together with the Soleus, which lies underneath the Gastrocnemius, these tendons pull on the Caleaneum (back of the heel) and are responsible for propelling the body forward (walking, jumping etc) while also stabilizing the foot when stationary.

These are the major muscles of the lower leg and, although there are more, they are all that you need to understand when beginning to draw. The other muscles (such as the Popliteus and the Plantaris) are largely subterranean and have little effect on the outer look of the leg.

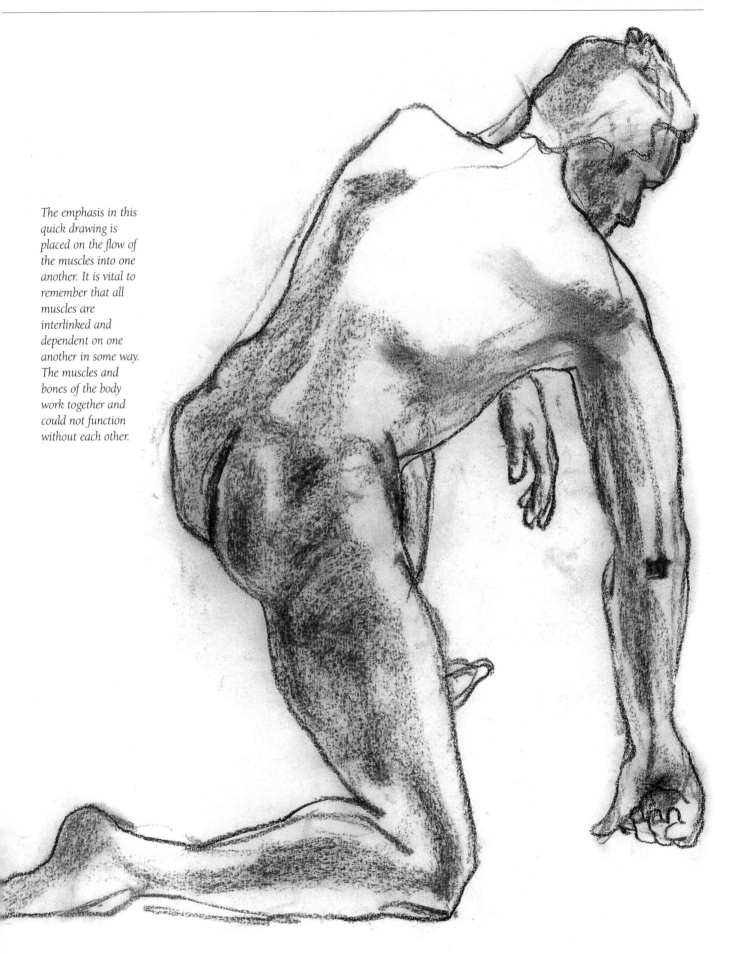

The emphasis in this quick drawing is placed on the flow of the muscles into one another. It is vital to remember that all muscles are interlinked and dependent on one another in some way. The muscles and bones of the body work together and could not function without each other.

Fatty Tissue

Covering many of
the superficial
muscles of the body
to a greater or lesser
extent, according to
the physique if the
individual, are the
various pads of fatty
tissue distributed
throughout the
body. The fatty
tissue is concen-
trated in certain
areas of the body
more than others.
The rear, hips,

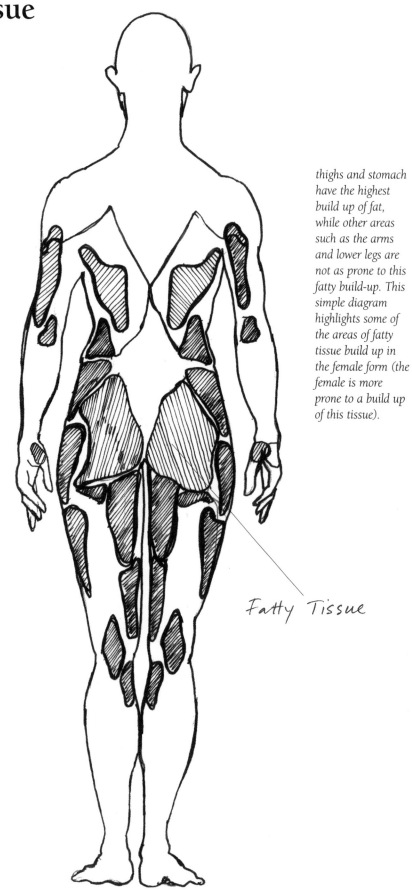

Fatty Tissue

thighs and stomach
have the highest
build up of fat,
while other areas
such as the arms
and lower legs are
not as prone to this
fatty build-up. This
simple diagram
highlights some of
the areas of fatty
tissue build up in
the female form (the
female is more
prone to a build up
of this tissue).

The extent and
location of fatty
build-up varies
greatly from person to
person (both male
and female) and as
such each body
should be observed
and drawn as seen.

The Hands

THE BONES OF THE HAND ARE DIVIDED INTO THREE CATEGORIES.
There are eight Carpal bones nearest to the wrist, five
Metacarpals running the length of the palm and in each
finger there are three planges (apart from the thumb which
has only two).

The Carpal bones form a cluster and are held together by
tightly binding ligaments. These bones are in place so that
greater movement of the wrist is possible. Because the
Carpals hinge on multi-joined sides and freely with each
other, the wrist can move through an entire circular motion.
This is vital to the function of the hand.

The five metacarpals form the major bones of the hand.
Two of these bones (the second and third – the thumb is
the first) are fused together and immobile thus giving a
steadiness to the hand. The other three metacarpals are
mobile and allow for the clasping of the hand.

The phalanges are the bones of the finger. They hinge on
the metacarpals and form the divisions of the fingers. The
phalanges can only bend towards the palm and cannot
rotate sidewards.

The most powerful muscles of the hand are those
operating the thumb. There are three muscles that create
the body of the thumb; the Abductor Pollicus Brevis, the
Flexor Pollicus and Adductor Pollicus. These three muscles
attach to the Flexor Retinaculum of the wrist and the
connected Carpal bones. They work together to rotate
outwards (abduction) and inwards (adduction) towards the
palm of the hand.

Opposite the thumb on the other side of the hand are the
muscles that control the adduction and abduction of the
little finger. The abductor digit works to pull the little finger
outwards, away from the palm of the hand, while the
opponeus digit and the flexor digit bring the finger back
inwards, towards the palm.

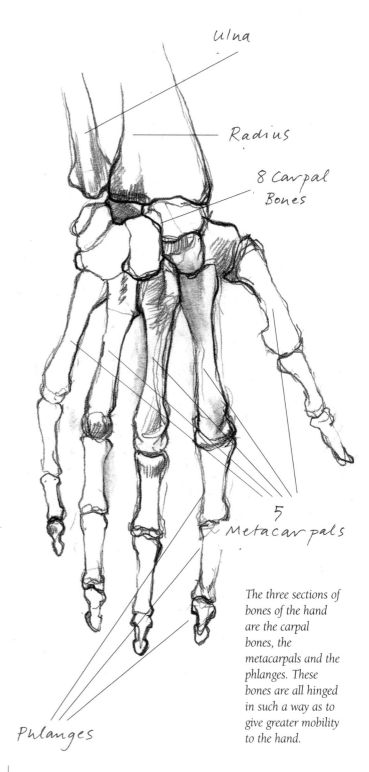

Ulna

Radius

8 Carpal
Bones

5
Metacarpals

Phlanges

*The three sections of
bones of the hand
are the carpal
bones, the
metacarpals and the
phlanges. These
bones are all hinged
in such a way as to
give greater mobility
to the hand.*

58

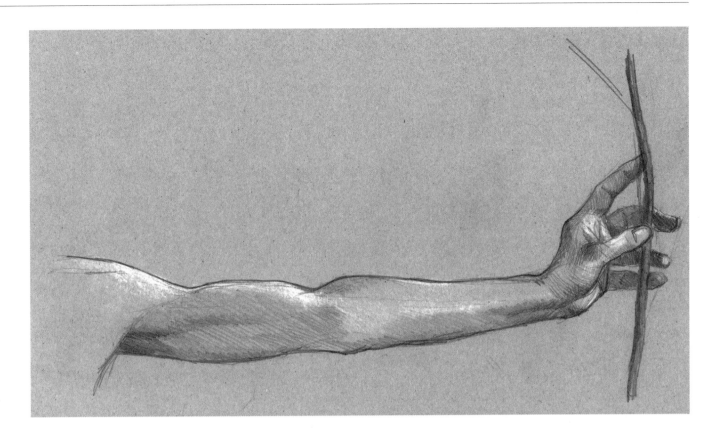

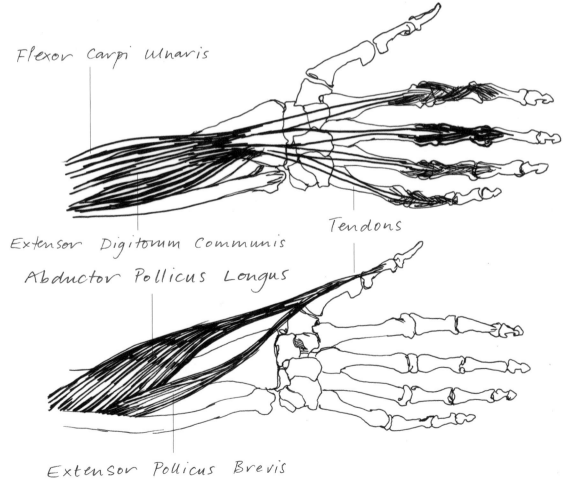

Flexor Carpi Ulnaris

Extensor Digitorum Communis

Abductor Pollicus Longus

Tendons

Extensor Pollicus Brevis

Each finger (including the thumb) has at least two tendons connected to muscles in the lower arm, running along it. These tendons with their respective muscles are what drive the tension and flexion of the hand. In total there are 30 tendons running into the hand through the wrist all contributing to the vast, precise, vital and varied movements possible in the hand.

The Hands

THERE ARE A SERIES OF MINOR MUSCLES FLANKING THE metacarpal muscles of the four fingers. These muscles are responsible for the abduction (opening/spreading) and adduction (closing/bringing together) of the fingers.

The muscles controlling the abduction are the four dorsal interossei. Responsible for the adduction of the fingers are the three palmar interossei.

Each finger (and thumb) has a tendon (with its origin in one of the many muscles of the upper arm) running along its upper and under side. These tendons act like powerful cables controlling the vital flexion and extension of the fingers. The tendons on the underside of the fingers running through the palm and underside of the wrist control the flexion of the fingers and thumb (the grip/clenched fist).

The tendons running along the upper surface of the fingers (clearly visible as they run over the knuckles and the top of the hand) are responsible for the extension of the fingers and thumb. These tendons can perform their function due to the contraction of the muscle at their origin when, during contraction, the tendon is pulled upwards along the arm, pulling the finger with it.

It is well worth observing the many movements of the hand before drawing them. While many developing artists find drawing hands troublesome, a little time spent drawing hands every day will erode this difficulty and replace it with a fascination and wonder that will never disappear.

Hands are everywhere
to be seen and a
journey on the train
or evening in the pub
will provide all the
drawing material
needed by the artist
intent on drawing and
understanding the
hand in action.

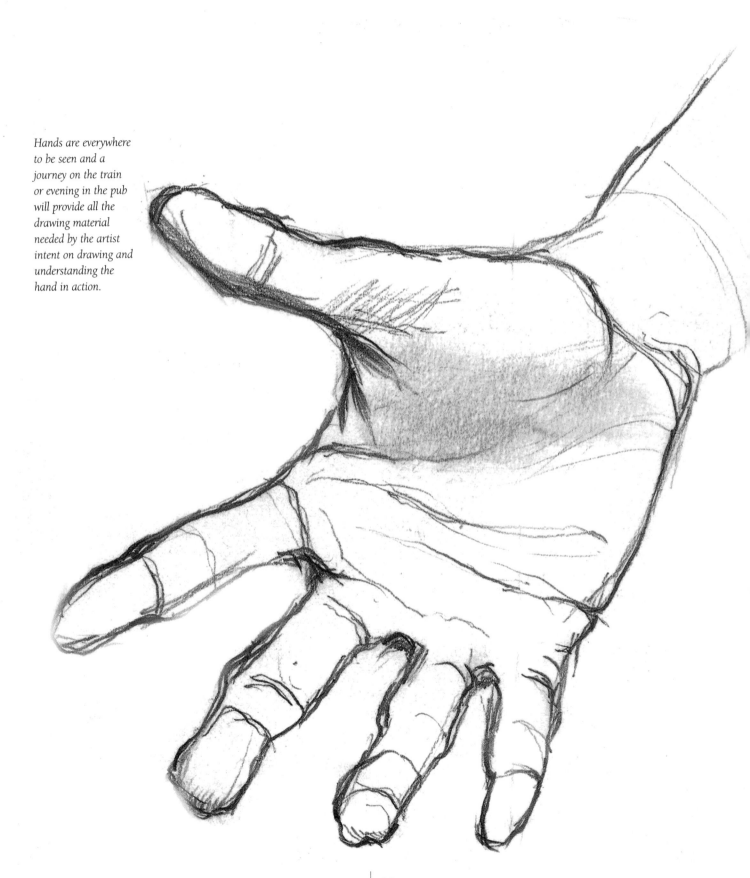

The Feet

THE BONES OF THE FEET ARE ARRANGED IN ORDER TO DISTRIBUTE the weight of the body and to act as powerful shock absorbers. This is achieved by two arch-like shapes, the first running from the heel to the toes on the underside of the foot with the second arch running across the bridge of the foot at the metatarsal bones.

While there are many similarities to be found in the appearance of the bones and muscles of the feet and hands, the main difference is one of function.

While the hand has been designed to achieve great dexterity, the foot is designed to make use of similar structural and muscular make-up to concentrate on providing stability and strength.

The foot is made up of seven tarsal bones (shock absorbers), five metatarsals, fourteen phlanges (toe bones) and a heel bone (calcaneus).

The calcaneus is the first bone to make contact with the ground while walking. It acts like a lever, raising the foot from the ground. When we are standing still our body weight is distributed evenly between the heel and the heads of the five metatarsals. When we leave a footprint in the sand it is these two points of the sole of the foot that make the strongest impression in the sand. As we move forward the weight of the body is placed more heavily on the heads of the metatarsals.

As with the hand, the main movements of the foot are controlled by long, powerful tendons running along the upper hand and lower planes on the foot. These cable-like tendons act exactly as do the tendons of the hand.

The tendons running along the bridge of the upper foot control the extension of the foot and toes, while the tendons running along the underside of the foot control the

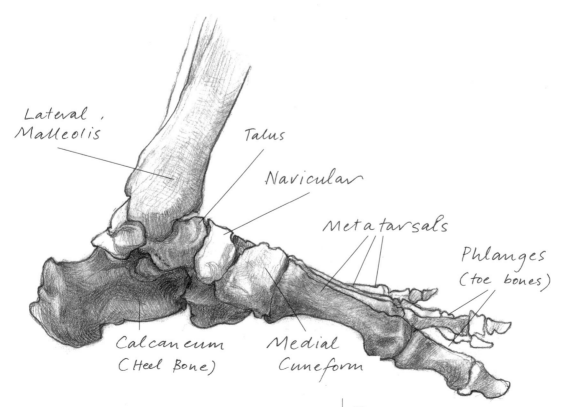

Lateral Malleolis

Talus

Navicular

Metatarsals

Phlanges (toe bones)

Calcaneum (Heel Bone)

Medial Cuneform

Structurally the bones of the foot are rather complex. It is easier to draw the foot when we understand their function. Primarily the bones of the foot give balance to the body and absorb the shock generated when walking or running. The heel bone (calcaneum) takes the initial shock. This shock is then transferred through the tarsal bones and into the metatarsals (the other major contact of the foot with the ground).

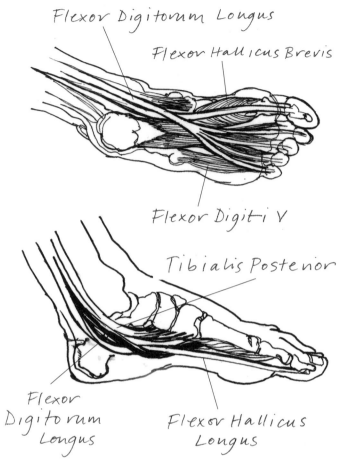

Flexor Digitorum Longus

Flexor Hallicus Brevis

Flexor Digiti V

Tibialis Posterior

Flexor Digitorum Longus

Flexor Hallicus Longus

flexion of the toes and foot. These tendons can be easily seen on the foot (particularly on the bridge of the foot and toes) as there are very few muscles operating along the 'roof' of the foot.

Most of the twenty intrinsic foot muscles are to be found on the underside of the foot. The most important of these muscles are the flexordigitorum brevis, the abductor digiti minimi, the abductor hallicus and the extensor digitorum brevis. These muscles work to extend, abduct, adduct and flex the toes.

The sole of the foot is protected by fatty connective tissue and hard skin. The connective tissue is vital in preventing the skin of the sole from moving excessively - without this walking might easily resemble a constant slipping on a banana peel!

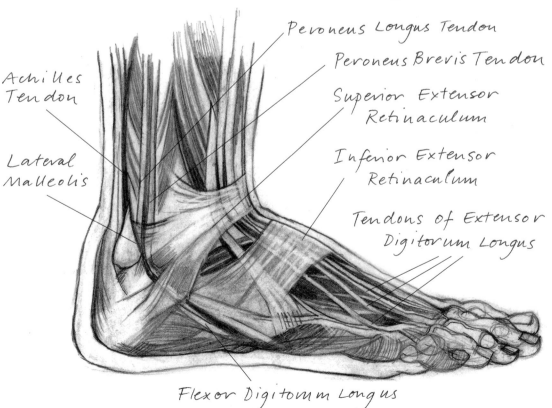

Peroneus Longus Tendon

Peroneus Brevis Tendon

Superior Extensor Retinaculum

Inferior Extensor Retinaculum

Tendons of Extensor Digitorum Longus

Achilles Tendon

Lateral Malleolis

Flexor Digitorum Longus

In many ways the muscles and bones of the foot operate in the same way as those of the hand. As with the hand, each toe has at least two tendons connected to muscles controlling flexion and tension. The main difference between the hand and the foot is functional. The dexterity of the hand is sacrificed in the foot and is replaced with a greater stability and strength.

USING
ANATOMY

Drama

It is not enough just to know the muscles, bones, anatomical structure etc., for their own sake. Anatomical knowledge is only useful to the artist if it is used to enhance the impact of the figure in the work of art. In this chapter I show some examples of how basic knowledge of anatomy has helped in bringing greater drama to drawing.

It is most important to remember when attempting to bring greater drama to your work that less is quite often more. Find out where the greatest tension and force is focussed on the figure you are drawing - this is often where the most weight or stress is being held. In your drawing make more of this point than you might initially be inclined to do.

The rest of the body should then be treated as the supporting cast to the main character.

Drawing involves choice and subjectivity. It is for you, the artist, to choose what it is you are going to draw out of the figure before you. Often you may be interested in a more subtle characteristic in a figure showing the grace of a dancer or the energy of youth. For this the same rules apply, and the process is still the same. Each body has its own language of movement and the challenge of the artist is to represent this with clarity and strength. Your understanding of anatomy will help considerably with this.

In both of these drawings the line used is carefully chosen to represent the character and unique drama of the figure. In these drawings the lines chosen are intended to be more feminine in character. Sometimes stronger 'found' lines are appropriate whereas at other times many of the lines making up the figure should be 'lost' so as to give the form greater flow.

Drama

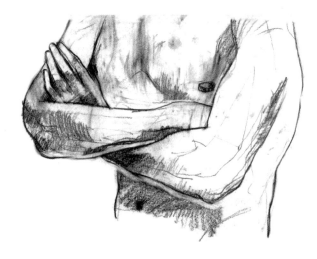

Tone, if used judiciously, can give a drawing a great deal of drama. Tone can also be used to draw attention to the form and structure of the body both in both gesture and anatomy. Locating the dominant light source and limiting your tonal range to just three tones will simplify the tonal drawing and give it the power and simplicity it needs to work as a drawing.

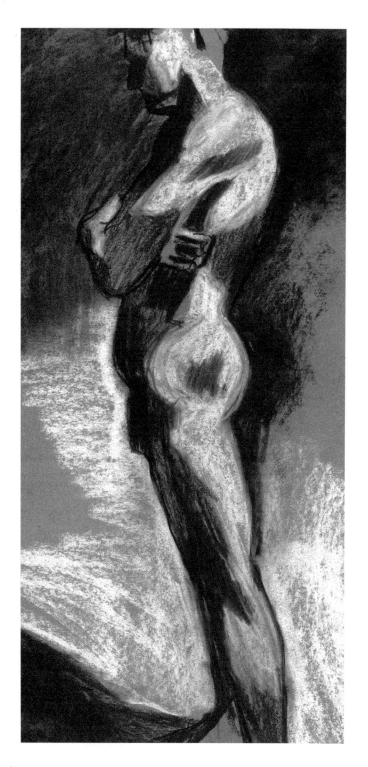

Distortion and Characterization

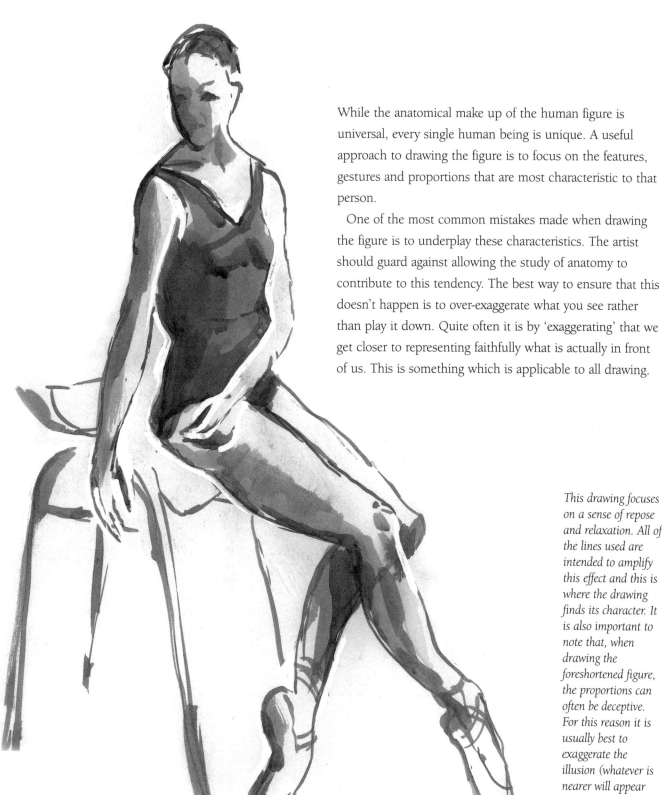

While the anatomical make up of the human figure is universal, every single human being is unique. A useful approach to drawing the figure is to focus on the features, gestures and proportions that are most characteristic to that person.

One of the most common mistakes made when drawing the figure is to underplay these characteristics. The artist should guard against allowing the study of anatomy to contribute to this tendency. The best way to ensure that this doesn't happen is to over-exaggerate what you see rather than play it down. Quite often it is by 'exaggerating' that we get closer to representing faithfully what is actually in front of us. This is something which is applicable to all drawing.

This drawing focuses on a sense of repose and relaxation. All of the lines used are intended to amplify this effect and this is where the drawing finds its character. It is also important to note that, when drawing the foreshortened figure, the proportions can often be deceptive. For this reason it is usually best to exaggerate the illusion (whatever is nearer will appear bigger etc) rather than underplay it.

Distortion and Characterization

I have heard it said that it is easier to tame a wild horse than it is to inspire a lazy donkey! It is the same with drawing. Rather exaggerate and then 'tame' your drawing after than try to bring energy and character into a drawing that was dull from the start.

Over the ages the 'ideal' for the human figure has changed over and over again. We can chart this change looking at the works of art to come out of each age. The Greeks favoured a balanced muscular yet lean ideal for the figure. The Italian Renaissance marked a return to this ideal by following a long medieval period where the human figure was not seen as an object of perfection or ideal proportion. As a result most medieval figures are not muscular at all and tend to draw very little focus to themselves. In even starker contrast we have the paintings of Rubens whose women are, by Renaissance standards, overweight. His obvious love of larger proportions was not only his own preference but also a fashion of his time.

Nowadays we receive so many messages from news and media, fashion and film that it is best to simply observe as deeply as possible what you actually see around you. A true artist is always ahead of the times, not because of being able to see into the future but as a result of the ability to see, objectively, well into the present.

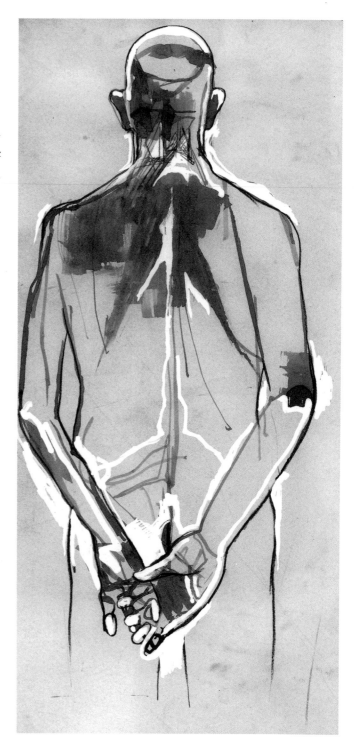

Knowledge of anatomical structure should be used to enhance and give personality to drawing. Often a drawing needs to defy anatomical 'sense' so that it may communicate the vision of the artist. By using line, tone and colour imaginatively artists throughout history have used drawings of the figure to communicate both the simple and the sublime.

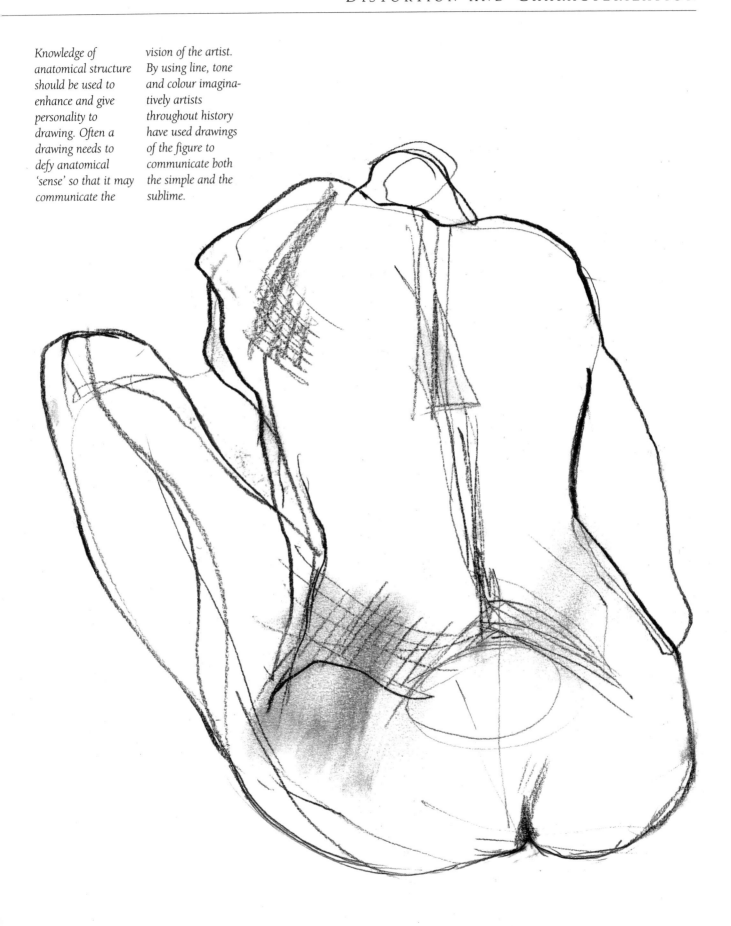

Learning from the Masters

ALTHOUGH, MEDICALLY SPEAKING, WE HAVE THE GREATEST understanding of the workings of the human body now than we ever had, there is still plenty to learn from the Great Masters who went before us. An entire book could be devoted to this section and I would strongly advise that any student of artistic anatomy consults the Masters, as this is an excellent and inspiring way of gaining a deeper and more fluent understanding in practice.

The main question is: "How do we learn from the Masters?" Obviously we can learn much just by looking at the drawings of the Greats (Leonardo, Michelangelo, Raphael, Tintoretto, El Greco, Goya, Ingres amongst many others).

There is a way of taking this study a little further though, and that is role play. You will need a willing and able assistant who is happy to pose partially naked in front of you. The next step is to find a drawing, painting or sculpture that you admire and would like to study further. Take the figure you wish to study and ask your assistant to take the same pose, holding it for at least 15 minutes while you draw.

In your drawing you should try only to find out where the muscle and bone tensions and relaxations are occurring. The aim is not to make a copy of the Master but to get a deeper insight into what makes their figures work so well. During this exercise you should attempt to get into the same position yourself. Feel how the body responds and then put that all-important first-hand knowledge into your drawing.

The only warning this exercise needs to carry is that many of the figure positions in these great works are either very difficult or even impossible to physically achieve! Often the figure is distorted or a gesture exaggerated for greater impact in the work of art. If everything in the Renaissance were anatomically correct it wouldn't have been very exciting. Some positions therefore are definitely not to be tried at home!

Perhaps the finest lesson we can take from studying the work of the Masters is to learn to have the courage to let only the desire for expression guide your hand.

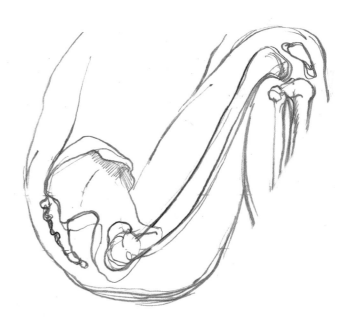

In this rather awkward pose all of the weight is borne by the upper part of the Gluteus Maximus. However, because the legs are pulled close to the chest, the Gluteus Maximus will be stretched tightly over the bones. This will mean that much of the pressure of the body will be placed on the Coccyx and the Ilium bones. Try this position for yourself so that you can feel the consid- erable discomfort this pose brings. This sense of physical discomfort is what gives much of the sense of isolation and tension expressed by Corot in this drawing.

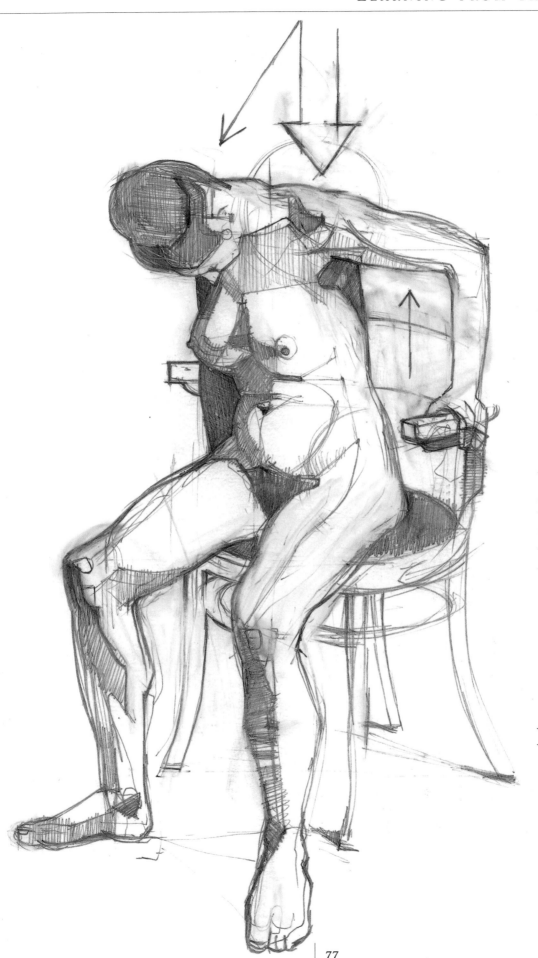

In this drawing of a painting by Euan Uglow we have a strong example of what I would call conflict of force. Although the primary weight (force) of the figure is downwards, there is an opposite force being exerted by the arm to lift the body off the chair. Uglow was a master at conveying comfort and discomfort in his figures and with this figure the discomfort seems to tell on the entire body. Most of the muscles of the legs, upper torso and arms are in tension and by using this to his advantage, the artist has given us a work of considerable energy.

77

Corot was a master of understated simplicity in his painting and drawing and in this copy of one of his drawings ('seated nude') we have a fine example of this expressive simplicity. Although there are very few obvious lines and tones showing the internal structure of the body, what is shown has been carefully chosen to ensure maximum expression.

Conclusion

It is my belief that the study of anatomy should involve much more than an attempt to analyse the human body like any other machine.

To truly understand the beauty, power, mystery and potential of the human form we must also attempt to know ourselves as well as those people who surround us.

More can be learned by looking at what is around us then by looking in any book.

A simple journey on the train, armed only with a sketchbook and pencil can be all of the anatomical tuition the artist needs, as long as there is real looking and enquiry taking place.

The magic is always there, waiting to be seen; it just needs the attentive artist to see it (or stumble across it…).

Good luck!